Welcome to issue one of SCENES Magazine, a publication focusing on all things classic and cult in movie land. I started this project because it was the kind of thing I'd be drawn to if I saw it online or at the magazine stand, it being full of interviews and articles on masterpieces and legends. This issue covers a wide area of film history, from the early silent years to the golden era and sixties onwards. From Chaplin and Keaton to Ettore Scola and Lindsay Anderson, there is plenty here to feast on for the cult movie junkie, and this will continue to be my aim in future issues...

- Editor, Chris Wade.

CONTENTS

I0462032

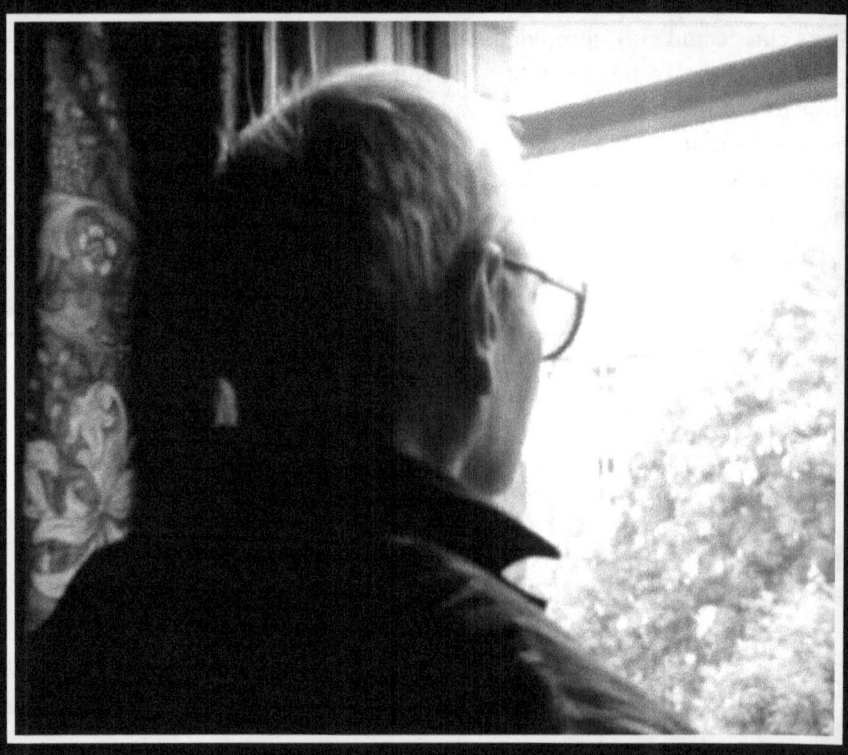

A LUCKY MAN:
LOOKING BACK AT
LINDSAY ANDERSON

Friends and collaborators look back on the
life and work of this great British maverick, known
for such films as if.... and O Lucky Man

Though film scholars and experts who are wrapped up in the overtly academic side of understanding filmmaking will no doubt find this special a rather simplistic look at the film work of British pioneer Lindsay Anderson, it is rather ironic that Anderson, though not automatically inclined to enjoy this piece if he were around today, might have at least appreciated the fact that the so called criticism here comes from a highly personal viewpoint. The article hopes to look at Anderson's work from a fairly straight forward angle, as a modern viewer far removed from many of the sociological and political issues of the time these works were filmed (though most are still relevant in modern society), appreciating both the aestheticism and, perhaps more importantly, the poetical symbolism presented.

In his influential Sight and Sound article entitled Stand Up! Stand Up!, published when he was writing about films as well as making influential documentaries, Anderson highlighted the sheer pointlessness of film criticism as it stood back in the mid 1950s (it was, in Lindsay's view, pretty worthless), and pushed for a committed form of both filmmaking and film criticism; concerned, political, class conscious, but most importantly of all, personal. "There is no such thing as uncommitted criticism, anymore than there is such a thing as insignificant art," Anderson wrote in that immortal piece, which he typically denied had had any kind of influence on film writing at all (it clearly did have). "It is merely a question of the openness with which our commitments are stated. I do not believe that we should keep quiet about them."

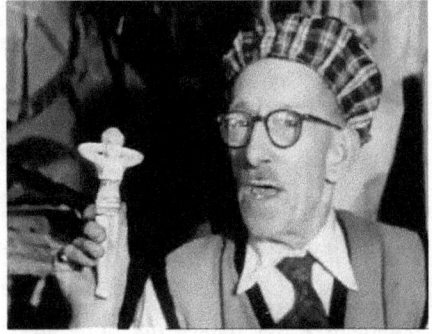

When I'm writing anything about Lindsay Anderson, one feels as if his immense intellect is ever present, mocking every syllable I put down, and I cannot help but picture the great man himself peering over my shoulder, just to see what it is about him and his work I have so clearly misunderstood. He'll be looking down his prominent Roman nose, judging and scrutinizing every

3

thought, every word I dare to type. At the same time, I feel that many Anderson scholars may be the same. There seem to be fewer and fewer Anderson devotees around these days, which is a shame, as the current mode of movie making needs men like Anderson, fierce independents with a conscience. My adoration for Lindsay's work is, I feel, justified and not a case, as had been suggested by one or two people in the past, a result of my supposed film snobbery. Anderson's poetic quality as a filmmaker, clearly his most important aspect, is unmatched; the man was a true artist, one who managed to be poetically pure without ever being pretentious. His habit of challenging the system and highlighting the rotten core of the English establishment and its obsession with class speaks to me personally, and makes one long for a new breed of Anderson crusaders, coming in to challenge the middle and upper middle class hierarchy of our society.

Lindsay Anderson was born in 1923, in Bangalore, India, the son of a high ranking military officer. When his parents split, a young Lindsay came over to England. He was a student at the public school Cheltenham College, in every way a product of Britain's stiff, immovable, hopelessly rigid traditional upper middle class system. As he was a man on the inside, Lindsay could see the decay within, the backwards mode of thinking which undoubtedly jarred with his own. He was an Oxford boy, graduating from Wadham College with a degree in English, before taking part in the last year of the war, working as a cryptographer for Intelligence. The strict leftist famously put up a red flag on the roof of the Junior Officer's building in Annan Parbat upon the victory of the labour party. Clearly, Anderson was intent on making his views known from the word go.

Lindsay's involvement with film began with criticism for his influential film magazine Sequence, which he started with Gavin Lambert and Karel Reisz. He then went on to write for Sight and Sound, a publication he later rubbished at any given opportunity. That said, few writers on film ever came close to what Lindsay achieved with his reviews, so one can argue that his crusade for a more committed film writing failed.

Anderson truly came into his own when he began making short

documentaries alongside Karel Reisz and others, showing them at the National Film Theatre, a group of films which later came under the banner of Free Cinema. Though Free Cinema as a manifesto was admirable, the movement made only a small dint in the British film industry, which rather than making the viewer think was more interested in entertaining them. "No film can be too personal," were the rules, "the image speaks, sound amplifies and comments. Size is irrelevant. Perfection is not the aim. An attitude means a style. A style means an attitude." These beliefs were far ahead of their time, and though Britain never fully embraced the idea of the art film as Europe did, Free Cinema did influence the British cinema for a short while, and certainly saw itself channel into the more popular realist films of the early 1960s, derogatorily, and rather patronisingly referred to as the "kitchen sink" movies. Anderson made some seminal films in this period, namely Wakefield Express (1952), O Dreamland (1953), and Thursday's Children (1953).

Though he was never truly a part of the British film industry of the 1960s, he did make one film which came under the "kitchen sink" tag, when he had the chance to direct This Sporting Life in 1963, a screen adaption of David Storey's popular novel, produced by Karel Reisz. Though not popular at the time, and coming at the back end of realist "working class" soaked cinema and the start of the swinging era led by the likes of Richard Lester and company, it was critically well received and is viewed today as a seminal movie, one of the best (and perhaps grimmest) films of the classic era of British realism.

Lest we forget, while Anderson was making a name for himself in film he was also a resident director at the Royal Court, where he oversaw the running of a number of groundbreaking plays, particularly those written by David Storey. As he stomped his way though sixties theatre, an actor's director in the truest sense, he went onwards in his cinematic work too.

Anderson's first feature led to commercials and trips abroad for commissioned films, but it was in 1967 that he established his own cinematic style with his screen adaptation of Shelagh Delaney's The White Bus; epic not mini, real but not realistic, symbolic as opposed to surreal. Andersonian

cinema meant personal, committed, conscious, satirical, savage, and anarchic. He was never a truly popular or fashionable filmmaker (he refused to admit he was ever successful on any level as a filmmaker, also denying to explain what success meant to him personally) but he was certainly influential.

In 1967 he filmed his most famous and celebrated piece of cinema, if.... (released in 1968), written by David Sherwin. This tale of public schoolboy revolt caused mass outrage, was a sizeable hit and even won the Palme D'or at Cannes, a prize which meant more than an Oscar to Anderson. "I'm making this for a few friends at Cannes," Anderson had informed the film's writer David Sherwin, and lord knows he must have been pleased as punch to walk away with the main prize. Sherwin, with typical wide eyed naivety, replied, "I'm making it for the whole world!" Lindsay would have likely tutted and rolled his eyes.

The film established him as a force of anarchy, a rebel with an acid tongue, someone who knew the privileged structure of England's ludicrous class system and proceeded to let off an explosive at its centre. When Mick Travis (Malcolm McDowell) and his gang of cohorts take to the school roof and unload machine gun fire down on everyone below, be they students, parents, teachers, clergy men, he was effectively symbolically letting off a hand grenade in the centre of England's heritage. Coming near the end of the sixties, if.... today has aged much better than most British cinema of the day, and that is perhaps because it never goes outside the school walls (save for one trip to a cafe on a motorcycle), remaining molecular, a microcosm of British society. This was the world Anderson knew too well (public school, "hell" as David Sherwin later referred to it) and he was not afraid to expose it. Fifty years later, with Oxford brats and their sort still running the country, if.... may be relevant but it also proves that while good art highlights unfairness and hypocrisy, it cannot change it. Still, the film has stood the test of time.

When Anderson went out into the world in his films, he never held back in satirising and tearing to shreds everything else about the country (and, effectively, the world at large) that irked him. In O Lucky Man!, the 1973 follow

6

up to if.... that came from a rough script from Malcolm McDowell (based on his days as a coffee salesman) Mick Travis (in name the same boy from if...., but not necessarily the same man, as Anderson

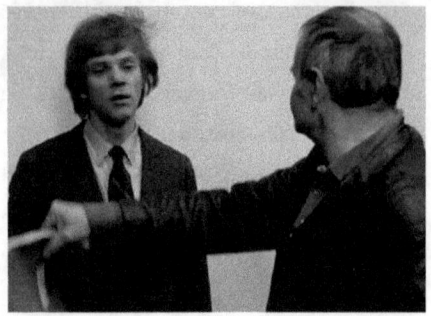

so often pointed out) is setting out into the world to be a success, to make his money and name as a coffee salesman in the north of England; but after experiencing the ugly side of what England has to offer and becoming a pawn and rap-taker for a corrupt upper class business monster (played by Ralph Richardson) he is imprisoned, and though battered he is far from defeated. Mick comes out with a new spin on life. Rather than striving for success, he becomes naively defiant on changing man's hatred for his fellow man. But again, he is greeted with such cynicism, even from those he is desperate to help, that his youthful and wide eyed outlook morphs into a world weary fatigue. In the end, he has to accept life for what it is, and comes to an understanding within himself. Rather than trying to change the world, Travis must merely adjust to its flaws and keep on keeping on.

In O Lucky Man!, both Mick and Anderson learned to accept the lack of humanity in society, and though the film is dark in parts, the finale has an uplifting quality which jars with much of Lindsay's other, more bleak works. In the follow up film (the last part of the Mick Travis trilogy) Britannia Hospital (1982), he took shots at everything he could, relentlessly so. The film itself is still sharply funny today and not without its fair share of outrageousness, but Anderson himself once said that its main flaw is that it targets so many aspects of society. In his defence, he probably got overexcited about having the chance to make another film (nearly a decade after O Lucky Man!) and went overboard. Seeing as films took so long to get together, Anderson later said that he took the rare opportunity to vent his spleen on screen and fit as much as he could into Britannia Hospital. In hindsight, perhaps he took on a little too much for one feature to hold. Though

the film criticises much of what Britain has to "offer", the NHS, privatisation, impatience advancements in science and the sickening fawning of the Royal Family came out most prominently in the savaging. As he approached sixty, Anderson had not calmed with age. In fact he was more vicious than ever.

While all this went on of course, Anderson was still directing successful stage plays, works by Alan Bennett and David Storey among others, and working with such actors as John Geilgud, Ralph Richardson and many more. Only a few of these were filmed (In Celebration, the 1969 play Anderson directed form Storey's play, was filmed for TV in 1975, as was Home in 1971 and The Old Crowd in 1979), which is a shame, for many feel Lindsay's true creative output was his work on the stage and it was there where he shone the brightest.

As the years went on, Anderson became less satisfied with film. He made pop videos, a tour film for Wham, and took on a few commissioned directorial jobs. He directed Glory! Glory! for US TV, but even though it was a success, he was surprised to not be invited back for more Stateside work on the small screen.

The Whales of August, a film he directed in 1987, was more impersonal than his more celebrated works, but he proved himself as a conventional film director on a more accessibly open level with the material put before him. He often criticised "popular" directors, knowing he was forever destined to be an "art film" director, but the truth is he was more than capable - if h really tried - of being a professional and taking to any project he found himself in, as long as he related to the subject of course.

Still, he was at his best when taking on personal film projects, and none were more personal than his final film, made for the BBC, entitled Is That All There Is? An ironic, funny and charming look at his everyday life, there is something slightly addictive in observing Anderson nipping over to the book shop, buying cheap wine (seven pounds proves to be unaffordable for him, and he opts for a £3.50 bottle instead), shopping in Sainsbury's, taking a bath while looking up almost fearfully at posters of his own movies, and dining with friends, most of whom are writers and actors, still hustling as Lindsay himself was. It was his swan song, filmed in 1993 a year before he died, and not broadcast until

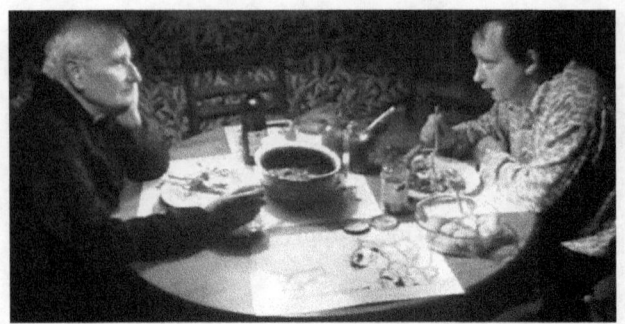

after his death. It proved somewhat poignant.

It seems a bit of a shame today, but Anderson's films and legacy are slowly disappearing into time. Sure, he has his fans, but most of them are quiet admirers, and his is not a growing cult of Kubrick-esque proportions. No doubt, if.... will remain an essential film for decades to come (it still makes top ten lists of best British films), but his importance and influence are lost on many young filmgoers. As Anderson noted, Britain has made us a nation of American movie lovers, and we still lap up everything the States has to offer (these days it seems to mostly be superhero films, which Anderson would have detested) while ignoring home grown dramas. The British films that do get an airing are primarily interested in "reality", either middle class comedies where so called eccentricities are celebrated in all their so called kookiness, or drab retreads of what filmmakers did during the early 1960s in the "kitchen sink" era, only the modern take is darker, more patronising to the working class and a prime example of superiority in the film industry. Anderson's poetic, class conscious cinema is a thing of the past, and very few - save for ageing old crusader Ken Loach and perhaps a small number of others - seem to be remotely concerted at what is happening to our nation.

In 1973, upon the release of O Lucky Man! Anderson declared it was a great time for satire, and that he was the only one doing it. Imagine then, what he would think of these modern times of austerity, greed and selfishness, the Conservative ruling, the persecution of the working class, the assault on the disabled, and the plight of the homeless man. We need Anderson more than ever. Unfortunately he is long gone, and no one looks to be taking over his rather unglamorous but extremely important place.

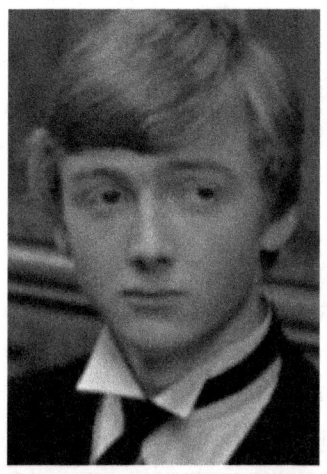

Q and A with Richard Everett
(Pussy Graves in if....)

Actor Richard Everett appeared as Pussy Graves in if...., his first film at the age of 19. Here he looks back on his memories of Lindsay Anderson and the making of the classic film.

Do you remember getting the part in if....?

Yes very well. I was about 19 and it was one of the first jobs I had as an actor. I was sent to read for one of the main parts which I didn't get but it was all very exciting. I thought it was going to be a kind of remake of Tom Brown's Schooldays - er, no! I wasn't nervous at all - there was me and Robin Askwith (Confessions of a Window Cleaner fame) and a few others at a casting director's office in Park Lane. We all came away very hyped up but with no idea what kind of movie it would be or even who Lindsay Anderson was at that time.

Do you recall your first meeting with Lindsay?

Yes, he was great - he had a wonderfully mischievous grin. I was immediately aware that this was no ordinary film maker, but an artist and someone who it would be enormous fun to work with. Also, as a young actor with no experience and far too much self confidence, I knew I was going to learn a lot.

What was it like to be directed by him? He had a lot on his plate on if.... with all the different age ranges of the actors and levels of experience.

I don't ever recall him getting stressed or agitated during shooting. Quite the opposite, in fact - and that mischievous grin was often there. At the same time, if you observed him closely you would

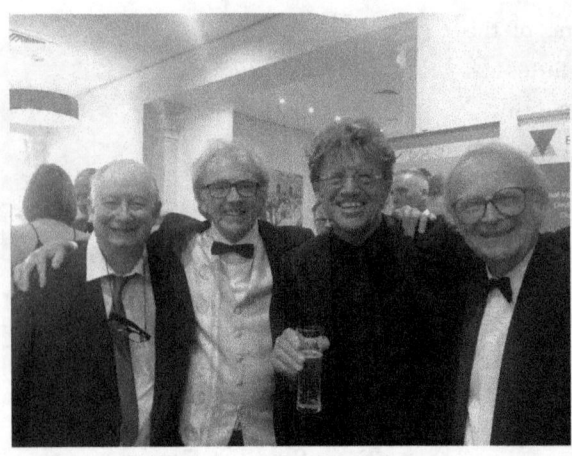

the script deliberately floating about but I don't think that incredible climactic scene was ever fully scripted - not that I saw, anyway!

Stephen Frears told me he knew it was going to be a popular film that affected people. Did you have any clue it was going to be so big?

also see him deep in thought, turning over an idea in his head, sometimes staring at the ground wrestling with another weird and wonderful possibility for a scene. And then he would look up, see you watching and grin that grin, and put his hand on your shoulder and ask 'How are you doing Richard?"

What are some of the stand out memories from the filming?

There were many. All the stuff on the army day when the chaplain gets shot was wild - none of us knew what was happening. And also the memorable final scene with Malcolm and co. on the roof top with machine guns was a shock to many of us - and deeply puzzling because there were various versions of

No not at all, but Stephen was much more experienced than many of us were. He was a delight to work with by the way, such fun on the set, I'm so pleased that he has become such a distinguished film maker and I'm proud to have worked with him all those years ago. But no, none of us really had a clue what kind of impact the film would have or even what we were involved with.

What do you think of the film now?

Well, like all great works of art, it has a timeless quality which makes it stand up well. That said, in terms of style it reflects the era in which it is made - Lindsay was a filmmaker and poet, but

11

also a man of his time. Some of the techniques therefore feel a little less subtle than appeared then. But it's a remarkable, ground-breaking movie and I am so proud to have been part of such an iconic piece of British cinema - I just wish I had appreciated that more all those years ago.

What about Lindsay, do you have fond memories of him?

Oh yes. What I will always remember about Lindsay was his generosity to actors. He loved them. Strangely enough, so many directors don't, and see actors as 'talking props' or as a necessary irritant (which they certainly can be sometimes). Lindsay genuinely loved the actors he worked with and kept in touch with them after the film was over and was a brilliant correspondent too. I still have a couple of letters from him - thoughtfully written and with great affection. I know many were on the receiving end of his generosity and he will probably be remembered for that by those who worked with him as much as the work itself. A true artist.

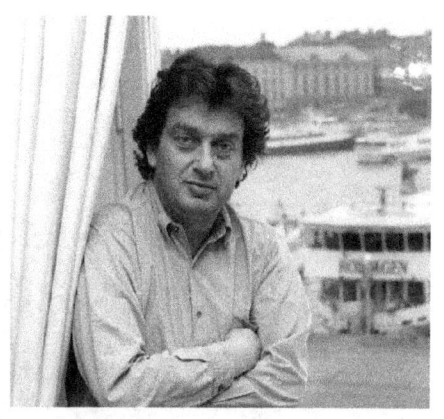

Stephen Frears
(Assistant Director on if...)

Today, Stephen Frears is recognised across the world as one of the industry's most reliable and consistently brilliant directors. Back in the 1960s however, he was an assistant at the Royal Court before working on if... as Lindsay Anderson's right hand man. I visited Stephen Frears at his London home in mid 2019 to speak to him about Anderson, of whom I was making a modest documentary at the time. According to film journo types, he is known for being a bit tetchy in interviews. I don't know what they are on about frankly. I found Frears warm, friendly, interesting and extremely accommodating. Though I used bits of

our chat in the documentary, this is the full interview, albeit a laid back one, in print.

Do you remember first meeting Lindsay Anderson?

I met him in Majorca. He'd gone out to meet Dan Massey to get him to work for him. That was the first time I saw him.

What do you remember from the first meeting?

Not very much! *(Laughs)* I used to go down from Cambridge to see plays at the Royal Court, and there I realised how brilliant he was.

So when did you become his assistant at the Royal Court?

I finished Cambridge in 63 and I became an assistant in 64. I was really an assistant to Anthony Page. Lindsay wasn't officially at the Court but he was there most days.

What kind of experience did you have with him there?

Well I was really out of my depth at the Court. I was a boy from the country, a boy from the provinces. But you had to have your champion. There were these brilliant men, Bill Gaskell and John Dexter. And Lindsay looked after me. So he was kind. But at the same time also shouty.

But you got on with him quite easy then?

Yes.

How did you get to be his assistant on if....? Did he just come out and ask you?

No, by then I had become a director. And then I must have been doing nothing. Maybe someone said, Can you come down and help?

So what did you know about if.... before going in?

I remember reading the script. I was working at Memorial Enterprises, Albert Finney's company, and I remember the script coming in. Well, I remember Lindsay bringing it in. First it was called The Crusaders, then Come the Revolution. Then a woman called

13

Daphne Hunter, who'd been Lindsay's secretary at the BFI said, Oh for goodness sake just call it if.... And it stuck. She just got cross and said call it if....

And he added the four dots?

Yes. And I remember at a screening... my then wife who edits the London Review of Books, saying, Should it be three or four dots? Are there four full stops?

Four, yes.

She questioned whether it should be four. I think she got a bollocking for that. And also for calling it a movie.

So he had already done This Sporting Life then hadn't he? And all the great shorts too.

Yes but I didn't know them. Gradually I got to know them, but I did see This Sporting Life at the time. This Sporting Life was in a cinema, you could go and see it, whereas Everyday Except Christmas wasn't. I thought all those

people were very clever and I liked that whole movement

So what were your jobs on if....?

I used to make those collages that are on the walls. David Wood said Lindsay used to make me rehearse with them or something ghastly. I was just around.

There are pictures of you somewhere doing all kinds of things...

Oh really? Of being useful?

Or pretending to be useful!

Pretending to be useful, yes. *(Laughs)*

So you were sat cutting the pictures out?

Yes I remember doing those collages. And when he shoots the picture of the Queen or Audrey Hepburn. I remember doing all that.

So you do you remember thinking that it was going to be a powerful film?

Oh yeah - and that it was going to be a very popular film too. I never had a

moment's doubt. There's a famous photo of a girl putting a flower down a rifle, which was of that moment. You just knew it was absolutely about what was going on at that instant. I never had a moment's doubt about it.

Some of it was actually filmed at Lindsay's old school wasn't it?

We filmed a lot of it at Cheltenham yes, and in North London. But a large part was done at Cheltenham.

Is it true that he wrote a fake screenplay to give to the headmaster?

Yes I think he did, but if you want my honest opinion I think the headmaster was cleverer than that and knew that it would be very interesting. So I never thought Lindsay had fooled the headmaster, I always thought the headmaster had been clever.

What was it like to watch Lindsay in control of a film like if....?

Well he was very straight forward. One of the problems is that he did not know the language of film. When you work on a film you work with technicians who work for 50 weeks of the year, so they know a hell of a lot more than you do. And because he had long gaps between filmmaking, it didn't come naturally to him in a way. I saw if... quite recently and I think the everyday bits of it are quite awkward. On the other hand the surrealist bits are absolutely brilliant. But he wasn't familiar with the language. And always the crew know far more than you. They just know an enormous amount. Lindsay never fully understood Miroslav (Ondricek, cinematographer of if....) and his use of lenses. He was always quite bewildered by what he was shooting. The thing with Lindsay was he was very much in favour of everybody else, i.e. me, doing any job that was going. They want you to make a cheap thriller, go and make it... everybody except himself!

Do you agree with him? Do you think that's a good bit of advice?

I think it is very good advice. I remember Jack Clayton saying, Don't be like us, don't wait five years to make another film... But I think that if.... is a terrific piece of thinking. I was always

less sure about O Lucky Man. I don't think I have seen Britannia Hospital, but O Lucky Man I was always rather dodgy about. I think it kind of peters out. That was what separated the men from the boys.

O Lucky Man is not as punchy is it?

No. And if... was very thought-through and told a good story and everything. There is a wonderful shot of a tall boy looking through a telescope looking at the girl leaning out of a window. And she's waving, you know. Absolutely fantastic.

Was all that kind of stuff all Lindsay's call?

Yes that would have been Lindsay. It is a wonderful shot. The surrealist stuff is terrific, much better than the clunky everyday stuff. He just had a very good mind, Lindsay. I think what he was, really, was a critic, and if.... was a piece of criticism on a very high level... on the country and everything.

Is it daft to ask you what you learned from Lindsay as a director for yourself?

I don't have a clue. I can never answer that question. Lindsay would say, Have you thought about this? He would make you think it all through. A lot of it was that I learned how to cast films. That came out of Miriam Brickman, a good friend of Lindsay's who was a casting director. They made you think it all through.

And trust your gut instinct?

Absolutely. If you haven't got instinct don't even start. Yes.

So then you began directing TV and film yourself, and you hired Lindsay to direct the TV play The Old Crowd, with you producing. That's something we don't get to read much about. What kind of experience was that?

The whole of LWT couldn't believe this man was coming to work with them. They couldn't believe what the implications were. We finished working at three in the morning. God knows how much it cost in the end. Lindsay became enormously entertaining. I will get shot for saying this but it's possible he was more entertaining than the work he was

doing. He was very sharp and funny. So the crew just couldn't believe that such a wonderful man had appeared in their midst. He was very dazzling. You see he was a military man, used to being in charge. He was very outrageous. Good for him. He would tell you what he thought. He wouldn't hold his tongue.

Did you stay friends after if.... and beyond?

Yes... the truth is I saw him on and off all through where our lives intersected. I had lunch with him about three weeks before he died. By then I had got to know Alexander McKendrick and he said, Oh I see you described him as a great man. He said, He should have backed us. I think that was something to with the Royal Court in the fifties. So this was in the nineties, forty years later, Lindsay was still feeling the same bitter edge.

The end portrait of Lindsay is often quite a sad one I think. He couldn't get much work in the film world...

You mean Lindsay?

Yes.

Well, I mean, I can't believe I get to keep on working. Yes. People would hire him knowing he was difficult, then he was difficult and they'd get cross. He would always present himself as being able to do anything, a western or a novel adaption, as if he could do something straight forward. But in the end he was directing plays in the West End. Maybe he could have done those films but they didn't give him the chance. Maybe he would have destroyed the opportunity in some way.

Lindsay used to say filmmakers are either poets or professionals, and he though John Ford was the only one who was both. Did he sometimes make it seem like he could be both too, like John Schlesinger or something?

God he was vicious about John Schlesinger.

I know, that's why I mentioned him!

(Laughs) Watch it! Yes, but actually, distinguishing between poets and

professionals... I am not sure about that. It's quite a trite observation for me, that.

Do you have personal favourite memories of if....?

Funnily enough things I remember most were things like Robert Kennedy being shot, hearing it on the radio on the way to work. You knew it was a film about what was going on. I mean, I have hit the zeitgeist now and then. My Beautiful Launderette hit the zeitgeist. But if...., it was very clear, to me at least, that this was absolutely relevant.

It seems Lindsay was a big name back in the 60s and 70s, whereas now...

Yes but that's a separate problem. He has a reputation among people my age. But I would imagine that younger people wouldn't have the first idea who he is. Maybe Lindsay just had a moment where everything worked. Lindsay did a few plays, all by David Storey and they were all magical. And I think if... was made around the same time.

Do you have nice memories of the latter period?

Yes I used to go and have lunch with him. We used to go to a restaurant together, but I would have lunch with him. By then videos had come in so his room was stacked with them. He was a very intelligent man, a brilliant man. I don't know anybody like him now. He was also a provocateur.

Comparing your career with Lindsay though, you've had a brilliant career, and been given so many chances to keep on making films...

But I wasn't difficult.

I was going to say, is it just the difficultness?

Yes maybe. And maybe I have different taste; my taste is more vulgar perhaps. But if you think of if...., for that brief moment he had it, he was able to juggle it all brilliantly. I remember Lindsay saying to me, quite late in life, For a moment I thought I could do it. I understood that. If it's working it should flow easily. Almost invisible actually, in a way Ford could have understood. You make films for people's pleasure, and any artistic importance is incidental. It's

about giving pleasure to the audience. So for me there has been times where I have felt it's good fun and what I am doing is the right thing. And then you go round the corner and it's not... So what I am really saying is that at the end of the sixties, everything Lindsay had been working for made sense. Everything came together at that point. Then it won the Palme Dor. Good for him. But you have to be lucky and on if.... he was lucky. I mean, you find Malcolm McDowell and you're lucky. But yes, it all came together. The audience were ready for him and he gave them what they wanted.

You don't think he has a legacy?

No, now he has no legacy. But I'm glad I knew him. In the end, it's the human things that matter.

I like that he wasn't a snob and seemed to be so kind.

Oh yes he was very kind. His flat was always full of people whose lives were wrecked. Jill Bennett and Rachel Roberts... He was like a refuge for them. But to me it always seemed like he was

celibate. He had a single bed, a room like a student. Like a sort of monk really. 57 Greencroft Gardens... He did live modestly, and that was how it was after all...

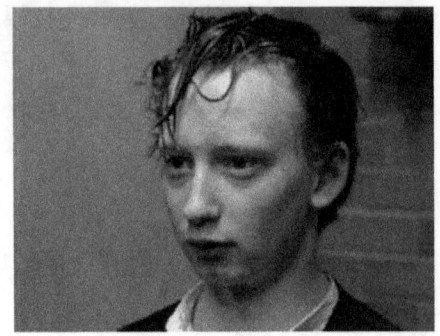

Brian Pettifer
(Biles in if....)

Brian Pettifer is an actor who made his film debut in if.... and went on to star in Anderson's O Lucky Man and Britannia Hospital. Staying friends with Lindsay, Brian appeared in his final film piece, Is That All There Is?, made for the BBC. Here he recalls working with Anderson through the decades....

Do you remember your first meeting with Lindsay?

Yes, the first meeting with Lindsay was in Half Moon Street. It was the office of

19

Miriam Brickman. I had seen her first and had a call and there was Lindsay. I had done a lot of telly up to then, but Lindsay was completely different. He was very friendly. He did not talk down to you. I remember it was raining and I had a cold, and he said, Put your feet up and get comfortable. That was very unusual for a director. So that was my first experience with Lindsay.

You were very young too weren't you?

Yes I was 17. I hadn't heard of Lindsay. I was a filmgoer and vaguely remember This Sporting Life, but didn't know much about him at all. But I got to know about him of course. I remember Lindsay saying, Oh Brian, you really should know about me. That was him!

What about your favourite memories....

Getting the part was the best memory, easily. I had never been in a film so far. And there were so many people up for the parts, and every time you'd go there'd be another hundred people there and I'd think, God, what's the chance of this? My agent was an American then, Tom Busby. He rang on a Friday and said, You got the job kid. So that was the best memory for me. Shooting was hard work. I met the younger actors first, but didn't see much of Malcolm, though I did end up working with him a few times later on and got to know him. The older actors kept themselves to themselves. It was just hard work. My main memories are of Lindsay being in control of everything. I had done a lot of tellies before that and most directors weren't really that bothered, but Lindsay certainly was. Everything had to be just right, but not to an obsessive degree. You know, not to a Stanley Kubrick degree or anything. We had a cinematographer who didn't speak English which was interesting. But he was a wonderful camera man, Miroslav. He died recently.

When you look at if.... do you see a Lindsay Anderson film or a collaboration with, say, David Sherwin or Miroslav?

No it is very much Lindsay's film I think. But David did write it, and had a huge input. That writing, ironic classical, there are some marvellous bits in it. I mean, the film has dated in certain

places but that's to be expected. But the look certainly hasn't dated, it's very good and of course the black and white and colour works. The performances stand up well as well. Graham Crowden and Arthur Lowe are fantastic; Malcolm of course too. It's a mix between the older characters Lindsay knew and the younger ones.

When you found out about O Lucky man, which came out a few years later, were you curious that you were playing Biles again?

Not really, no. It was just a bit disappointing that I wasn't in O Lucky Man more, but the character just didn't figure in the film. It was such a sprawling film. I don't think many of the if.... boys were in it. I was lucky to be in it, that Lindsay wanted me in it and that David wrote some scenes for me. I wanted to be in it more, because it's my favourite of the three. I'm in the coffee factory and then the prison section, which we shot up in Glasgow. I was going to be the pig boy at one point, which would have been great. They put me in the costume but it was too large and didn't fit right. I should have

complained and said, There must be a way you can make it fit, because it's such a great scene. Jeremy Bulloch plays it well. I am sorry it isn't me though.

Did you sense Lindsay was as in control on O Lucky Man as he had been on if....?

No because it was so sprawling and there was a gap in filming. There were all sorts of problems, because it was a much bigger and more ambitious film than if...., which I feel was much more modest. O Lucky Man was quite a task for a director. I had much more to do in Britannia Hospital. I was very disappointed in the reception it got. I always think when you are in a film you think it's going to do really well. But people hated Britannia Hospital, everyone hated it. Not everyone of course - they liked it in Argentina and France... I saw it six years ago and it was quite full and the film has held up quite well. There are some bits you couldn't film now, which is a shame. The slight problem with it is that there is no central character. Malcolm is in it but he gets his head chopped off. It was also criticised for being cast mostly from TV, but the budget was such that we weren't

going to get Robert Mitchum in it or anyone like that.

It's a great cast though.

It's a terrific cast, but it was criticised. Lindsay did rub people up the wrong way though. They displayed their opinion of the film and him. EMI hated the film. Lindsay went out for a screening with a head guy at EMI and they never mentioned the film, not a word, and then dropped Lindsay off in the middle of nowhere in the pouring rain to make his own way back. That's it, it's a tough business.

How did Leonard Rossiter and Lindsay get on?

Leonard had been in This Sporting Life. The part was originally for Arthur Lowe, but Arthur was doolally by then and could not have played that kind of part, though he is in it briefly. I don't know how Leonard got involved. He was popular then though. I don't think Lindsay's relationship with Leonard was anything like the one he had with Arthur Lowe but they got on well. I don't think they would have become firm friends though, but he was great fun to work with, Leonard. Everything was a gag to him.

You were saying there's no central character in Britannia Hospital but in many ways I think your character is the kind of main one we focus on.

I like that. Sounds good to me. It does run through the film, my part, but a main one the audience can relate to, I suppose is Leonard's part. But then again he does batter a guy to death with a spade. And Malcolm... whenever a star like him is on screen, you only want to look at them. He has that quality, Malcolm.

You were also in Lindsay's Is That All There Is? weren't you? You must have stayed good friends with him.

Yes I saw him frequently. I did stay friends with him. I saw him every few months or so. I was working at the National and would see him most days, though he was directing a different play. Yeah, and then we did is That All There Is? which was terrific. It was very good and very honest. The BBC took a long

time to show it and sod's law I think they showed it a few days after his death.

There's that great scene around the table with you, Lindsay and his nephew, when he ends up pouring the wine over his head...

Oh yeah. That was all planned but it had actually happened. I wasn't there though, but we re-enacted it. We did it in one afternoon or something. It was a good thing to be a part of. There were so many people in that film - actors, writers... a nice piece of work. It's deceptively simple as well. It was very ironic. I know Alan Bennett said the cross cutting between starving people and Sainsburys was very old fashioned but it was a fact and still is. There are starving people. It's still a reality for some people.

Do you think we need directors like Lindsay?

There is an audience for films that reflect the times but these days I don't know. Young people are not interested in having a mirror showing what's wrong. But I think it would be great to have more directors with a social conscience. I'd like something with a bit more teeth....

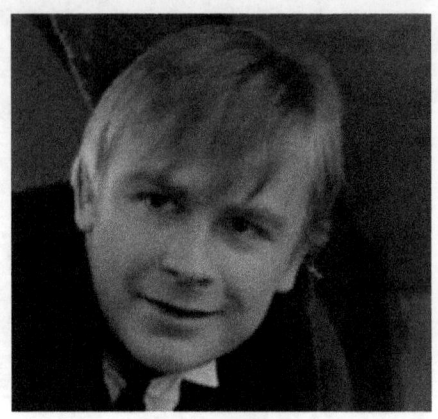

**David Wood
(Johnny in if....)**

David Wood had little experience on camera when Lindsay decided to cast him in if.... as Johnny, one of the three main boys. Speaking to me in 2019 for my documentary on Anderson, David recalled those heady times with joy.

Do you remember first meeting Lindsay?

Yes I was going to the audition. I was coming up from the tube to the Garrick Theatre and I immediately fell and split my trousers all the way from the crotch to the knee. It was quite good actually

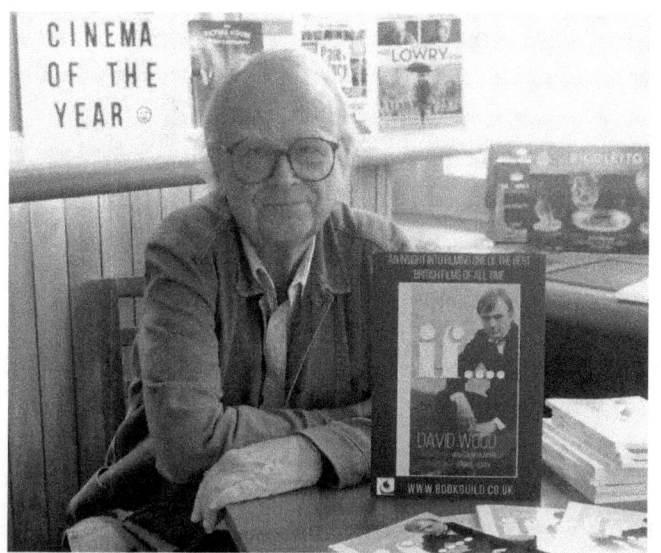

stayed there for two hours, reading all sorts of parts with all sorts of people. They said thanks and I got the train back to Worcester where I was doing a play. A few days later and another message comes through asking if I'd be able to come up for another audition. Somehow I got a hold of Lindsay's home phone number. I went to a call box under the stairs of the stage door area and I put some coins in, and I rang this number and he actually answered. He was very gracious.

because when I arrived it was a kind of cattle market audition. I was introduced to Lindsay and the first thing I said was I split my trousers. I don't know whether he found it amusing or whether it engraved me into his memory, I don't know. This group of us read and he talked to us a bit. He asked me questions. We'd both been at Oxford, he picked this up. He asked me about the word epic, what I thought of it, and I tried to be intelligent and mentioned Brecht and all this. I don't know if I said the right things or not but I did answer him. I thought that might be it. But I was asked to stay on longer because some people hadn't turned up. I didn't think it was because they were interested in me. I

But you got the part...

Yes. They asked if was I available on Sunday, and I was. They asked me to come up to this studio in Soho. They were looking for someone to model the school uniform. I thought it was odd that they'd asked me to go all that way. But I went and arrived. They put me in the costume with the tail coat and so on. They started taking photos. Lindsay was

very nice. He said, This is a bit boring, why not look at the camera as if you hate it? I had no idea this was a film test. So I went back to Worcester. Next thing I heard was I had a part. The part was Johnny. Then I went for a lunch with Lindsay and a few other people. Malcolm was there, and the lovely Richard Warwick too, and some production people, and we had a meal. I realised I hadn't had a script yet and the other two had. I didn't say anything and just kept nodding appreciatively. Then Lindsay said he wanted us to start collecting pictures from magazines to put on our study walls. I hadn't been to public school so I didn't know anything about this. I thought, I wonder if he means pictures *I'd* put up or ones my character would. I didn't understand at all. I went back on the train a bit bemused. Eventually they sent the script and I found out it was one of the main three boys. But it was a torturous process, though enjoyable.

A lot of people have said they found Lindsay intimidating, but he seems to have been more relaxed with you.

Maybe because I split my trousers and it relaxed him. No I didn't find him intimidating. Though directing on the floor I could see he was very single minded. And the pressure on if.... was considerable because the schedule was punishing for them. For Lindsay it was pressurised but again I never heard him lose his temper. But he was well aware that he had an extraordinary mixture of a cast. I think he was aware that he had to be careful not to treat everyone in an extreme professional manner, so he wouldn't get angry with people unless there was a point to it.

Did you get to know Lindsay off set?

Not really. I think he was a private man in many ways. I think when Gavin Lambert outed him years later (in his memoir which went into intimate details regarding Lindsay's sexuality) - that was unfair really. I don't think there was any question of Lindsay having been a corrupting influence. I think he was celibate. We know that he tended to put extreme heterosexual men on to a pedestal, certainly Richard Harris and certainly Malcolm... And it was as though he respected them and indeed

loved them. It wasn't flirtatious in any way, though we all knew Malcolm was the favourite. One totally accepted that, for he was playing the main role; though we were a little disappointed when if.... went to Cannes and Richard and I weren't invited, though it was very significant that Malcolm *was* invited. But Malcolm was determined not to take TV or stage roles after if.... because he wanted to get into movies. And we all knew he was special and weren't surprised when he became a star.

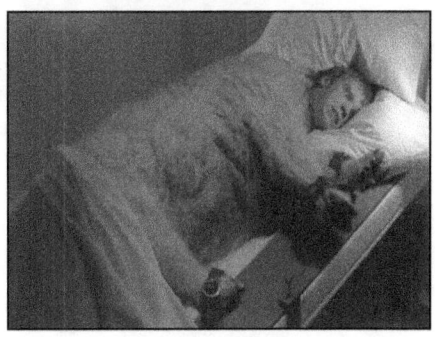

Jeremy Bulloch
(Pig Boy in O Lucky Man!)

In the world of Lindsay Anderson, Jeremy Bulloch is best known as the weird pig boy in O Lucky Man. Of course he does appear in the film three times; firstly as the smug driver of a sports car who over takes Malcolm

McDowell and then meets a bloody end, and at the end of the film as a man looking for stars in the busy streets of London, but most memorably as the afore mentioned victim of Dr Millar. In 2011 I asked Jeremy a few questions and he recalled his stand out memories of working with Anderson.

You had had quite a long career by the time O Lucky Man came along in 1973. How did you come to be cast in the film?

I had worked with Lindsay Anderson before on a commercial as well as being asked to be in the theatre production of Rosencrantz and Guildenstern.

What was your view on Lindsay Anderson when you first met him?

I liked him immediately. I got the impression that he had to be comfortable with the actors around him.

When you read the scene when you would be playing the pig man in the bed, what were your initial views?

I didn't realise exactly what I was going to look like in the hospital ward. Even to

this day people remember that scene of me with my head grafted on to a pig's body.

Where do you think O Lucky Man stands in Anderson's career and as a part of British screen history?

Lindsay had already proved himself both in film and theatre. The film was both praised and criticised. I had worked with Malcolm many years before in a soap opera called "The Newcomers." I enjoyed my time on the film with some great actors and I felt honoured to be part of it.

Do you have any funny stories regarding the making of the film?

No really funny stories except at the very end of the film when I had the sandwich board. I stood outside the cinema in Leicester Square as the public came out. The camera was hidden and Lindsay asked me to approach the cinema goers. I was there for hours. I was punched but not hard. What hurt me most was the way the general public swore as I walked towards them. F Off! You filthy F!!cker! Get a bath!!! At the end of the night shoot Lindsay asked me

what he thought of the reaction I got. I said that I got the response I expected. Lindsay stood looking at me and finally he said "I think we'll come back tomorrow night just to get the right look when you turn towards Malcolm." I couldn't believe it but Lindsay was right in the end. The final look to Malcolm felt just right. I wasn't looking forward to returning to the Leicester Square Odeon but luckily I didn't get too much verbal abuse.

I was about to ask if it was true that you got punched in that scene...

I was hoping that Lindsay would not entice people to punch me and film it. That would be physical abuse.

Finally, how do you look back on O Lucky Man as a film?

As I mentioned before it was both praised and criticised and my part was the alter-ego of Malcolm McDowell's character.

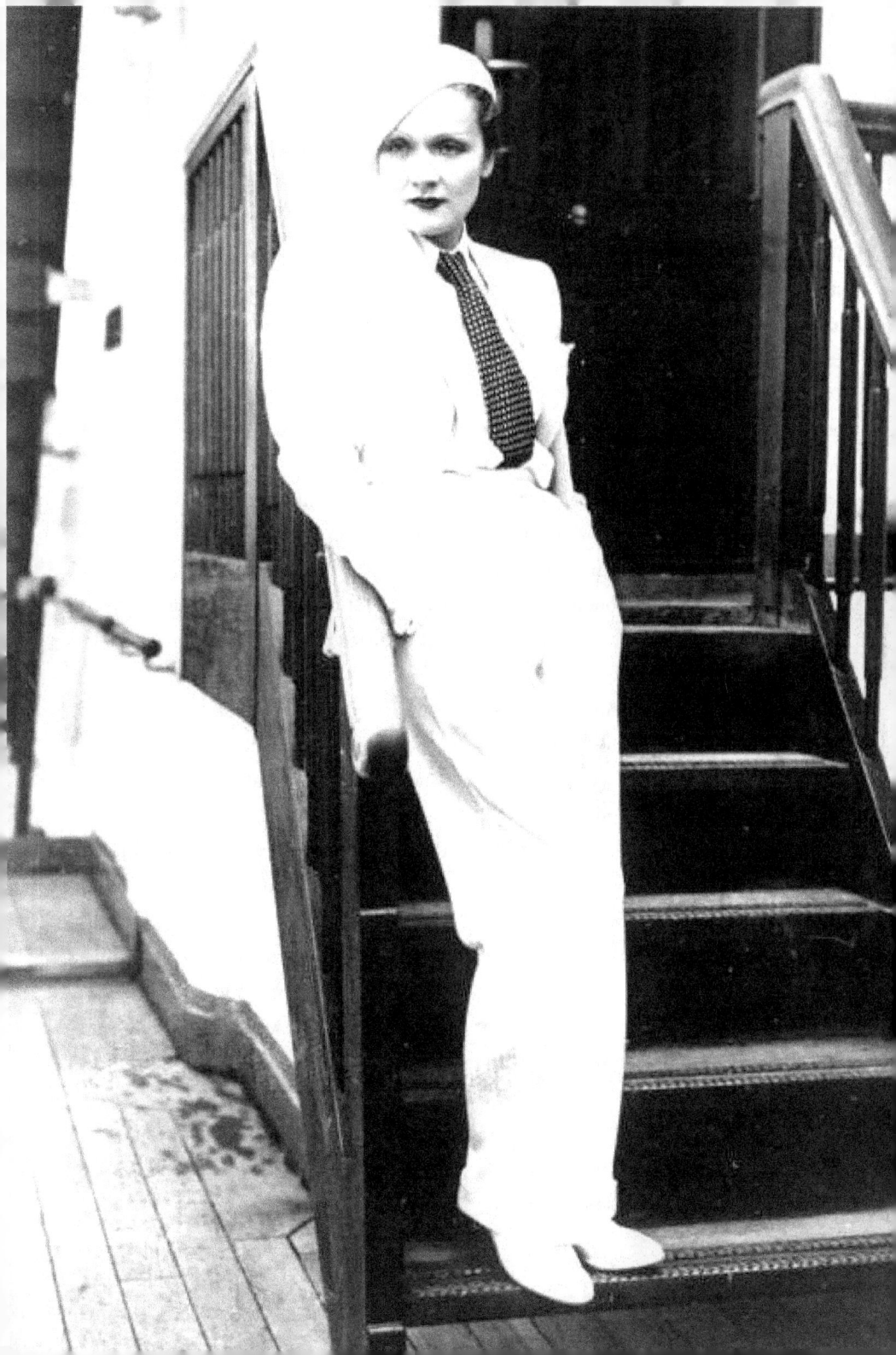

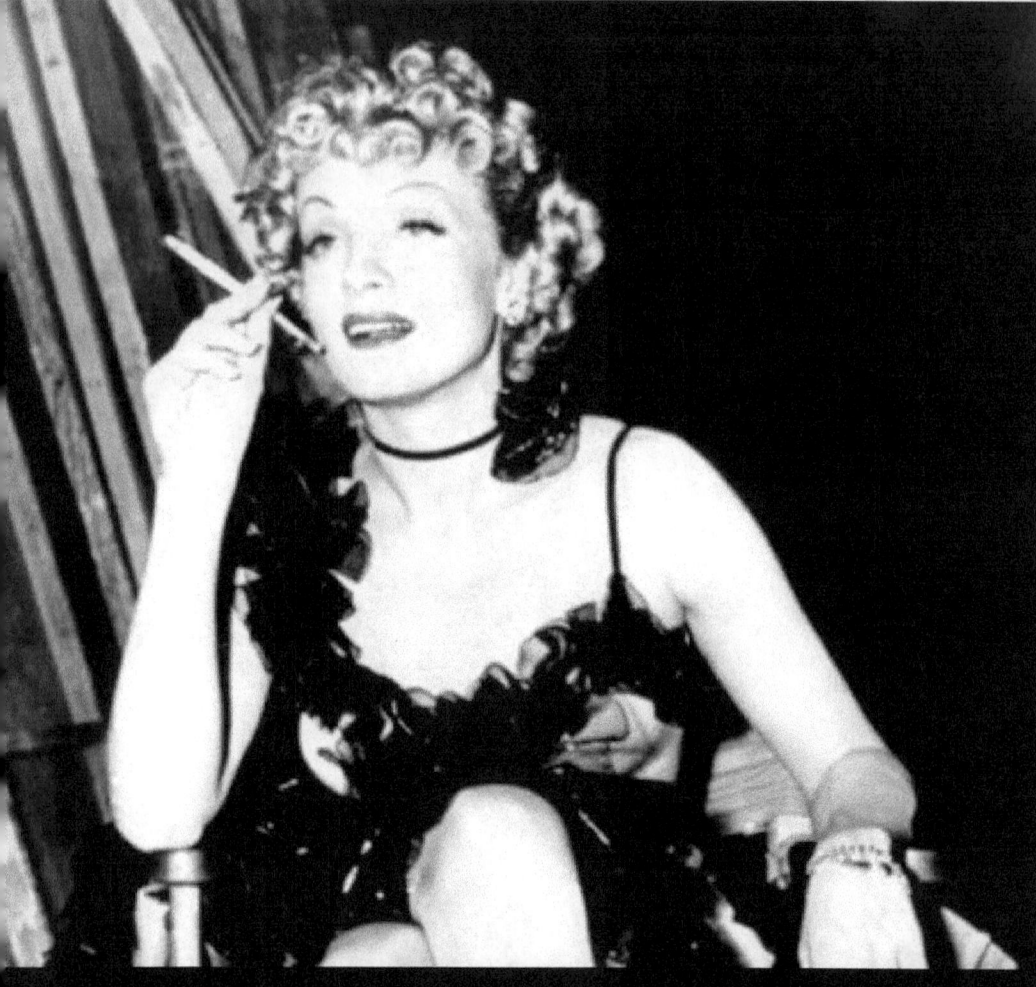

MARLENE DIETRICH
THE GODDESS OF GLAMOUR

ONE HUNDRED YEARS ON FROM HER
FIRST FILM APPEARANCE, CHRIS WADE
SALUTES THE CHARISMATIC SCREEN
PRESENCE AND IMMORTAL SEX APPEAL
OF THE GREAT DIETRICH...

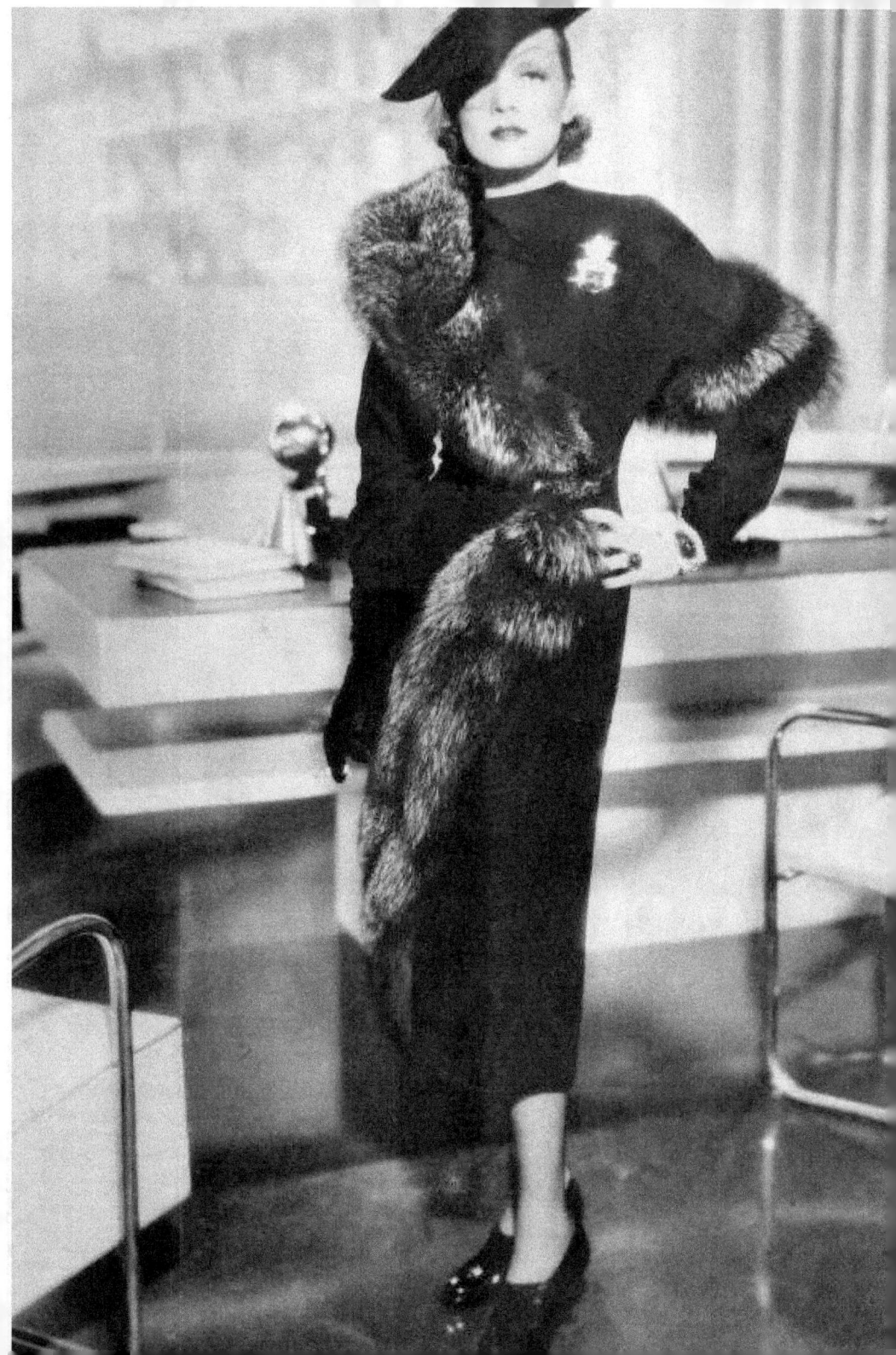

When exploring the film career of Marlene Dietrich, one is not accessing performances of extreme complexity, of subtle nuances and developments; one is simply enjoying heightened, stylised magic. Yes, Dietrich was a fabulous presence in the movies' golden era, but she was primarily a star of the screen (and stage of course), known for her glamour, larger than life exuberance and seductive appeal. In her day she was a mega star, though these days awareness of Dietrich varies. Older generations may remember her from when she was still around, popping up in brief cameos, many nods to her illustrious past; films buffs will know her from her work with Josef von Sternberg, those classic movies from the early thirties; younger generations may know the name and face but nothing else; while some, regrettably, will be absolutely clueless about her. This is of course inevitable, for the passage of time sees that world famous legends soon fade away into obscurity. But some stars of the past deserve to stay relevant, not just for the work they left behind, but their importance and impact on culture. For me, Marlene Dietrich is one of them.

Dietrich had already become a star of Germany's stage in the late twenties before her first worldwide film hit, 1930's The Blue Angel, made her a worldwide fascination. With director Sternberg they delicately crafted an image of sensuality, not just by careful lighting and costume, but also presentation. Think, for instance, of when she first appears in 1932's Blonde Venus, swimming naked in a lake, ogled by a group of men while she and her liberated friends frolic in the water. And who could forget the iconic moment in 1932's Shanghai Express, when she stands quietly, lit from above like a sensuous angel smoking a cigarette? This picture, with Marlene as glowing goddess, has become one of the most enduring images of the golden age.

Marlene captured the world's imagination through a deadly, enrapturing combination of factors, namely her glamour, her exotic classiness and her sex appeal. But Dietrich sensuality was not displayed distastefully. Unlike today's female stars, who display their sexuality and scantily clad bodies gratuitously, just as present Hollywood requires, Marlene teased the audience, keeping herself at a certain

distance but unveiling just enough of her mystique to hook the viewer from her first moment on the screen to the very last. Indeed, watching a Dietrich film is rather like being under a spell, and one cannot help but be seduced by the illusion, as carefully worked out as it may be, by both Dietrich and her directors. As manufactured as her image may have been, one never gets the feeling of being tricked or duped; more hypnotised, won over.

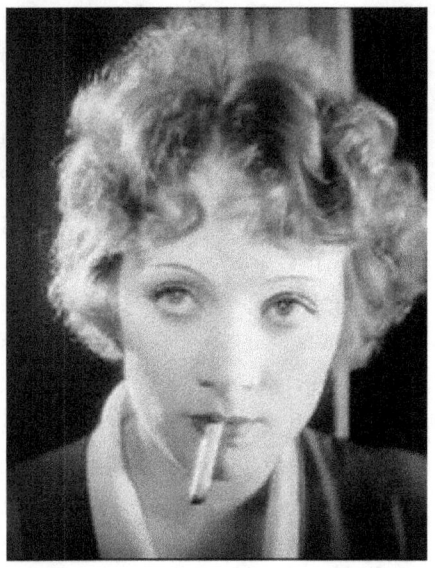

The earliest part of Dietrich's on screen career is often forgotten these days, people choosing to believe that she exploded out of nowhere straight on to the screen in Josef von Sternberg's The Blue Angel, the role that made her a star. In reality, she had appeared in nearly twenty German silent films before Hollywood had even heard of her. Granted, in these strange surroundings she is not the Marlene Dietrich we know from the golden period of thirties Hollywood. Yet when given more than a walk on part, such as in Cafe Elektric, she harbours star power and still commands the screen whenever she appears. The last two films she made before becoming a fascination were The Woman One Longs For and Ship of Lost Souls (both 1929), setting her up for The Blue Angel.

Her first film with von Sternberg may be rather stiff today, but that's because movies were only just out of the silent era, and miking up actors was still a tricky business. That said, whenever Dietrich hit the screen, either in the dressing room mentally terrorising her middle aged admirer Emil Jennings, or singing Falling in Love Again, she was hypnotically brilliant. Her subsequent and pretty sudden stardom does not seem surprising in retrospect. The camera loved her from the word go.

Her first pictures in Hollywood, again done with von Sternberg, remain

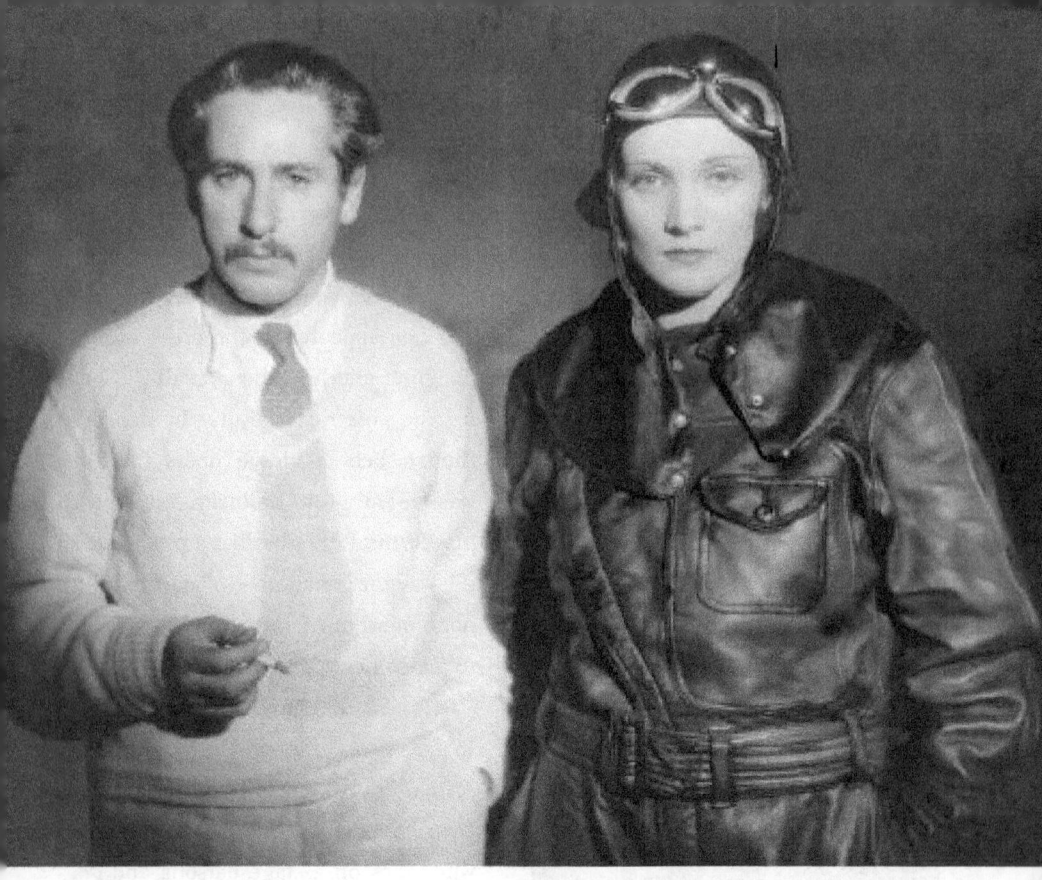

curiously watchable, though still rather odd in parts. There is a rigidity to them, a lack of cinematic over the top theatricality; indeed, they are often muted, but this may have been done on purpose so the viewer fell even more under the spell of Marlene. Morocco, released shortly after The Blue Angel, was just as iconic as its predecessor, featuring among many other memorable moments the scene in which she performs in a top hats and tails, and steps out to kiss a female member of the audience. Shocking at its time, Marlene was merely doing what she felt like and what was accepted in the more laid back Germany she had come from.

Dietrich's film career is in a way defined by moments rather than films, but in all the 1930s films every scene she has on screen is memorable, and in each one it is impossible to take your eyes off of her. In Dishonoured, released in 1931, she consolidated her fame and popularity with another fine turn as a female spy, in a film which seemed to

fetishise Marlene even more. Clearly, von Sternberg was just as intoxicated by his goddess as the film going public.

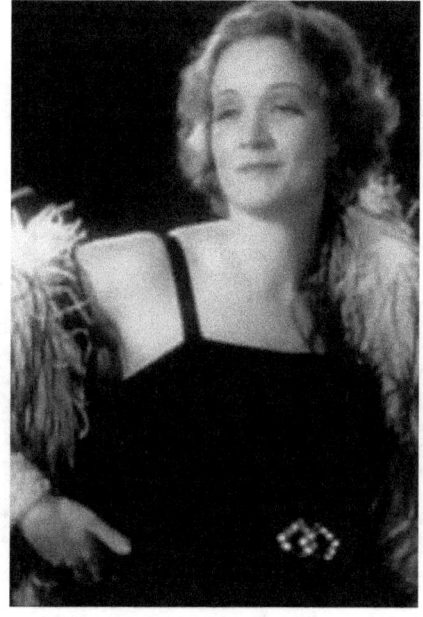

In my view, and the views of many others, Shanghai Express is the highlight of Dietrich and von Sternberg's collaboration, a strange and often surreal adventure drama set on a train that is taken over by rebels. Dietrich is the sultry Shanghai Lily, looking at her absolute best and delivering a charismatic turn that dominated the film despite her making very little effort, at least seemingly so.

By 1932 she was at her height. She was cool, suggestive, transgressive, light years ahead of her time in the way she fused sexuality, mystery and myth. At the same time, she was an adored star of the era and viewers felt like they knew her. She appeared in the press with her daughter and husband as if all was good in the Dietrich family home, even though behind closed doors their life was anything but ordinary. Yet Dietrich played the PR game like a pro, clearing the way for generations of stars to follow, none of whom I might add could hope to match her appeal.

Released the same year as Shanghai Express was Blonde Venus, a close second in my view to being the ultimate Dietrich experience. She plays a woman who takes on a stage persona and goes back to performing to raise money for her husband's medical bills, and meets dashing Cary Grant when doing so. She ends up in debt, in a lot of trouble and on the run across America with her son, a fugitive always looking over her shoulder. Thankfully she gets to Paris and rebrands herself as a star, in the end tying all loose ends and reconstructing her broken family unit. In some ways Blonde Venus has Dietich at her best, and she expresses more range than she does in the other von Sternberg films,

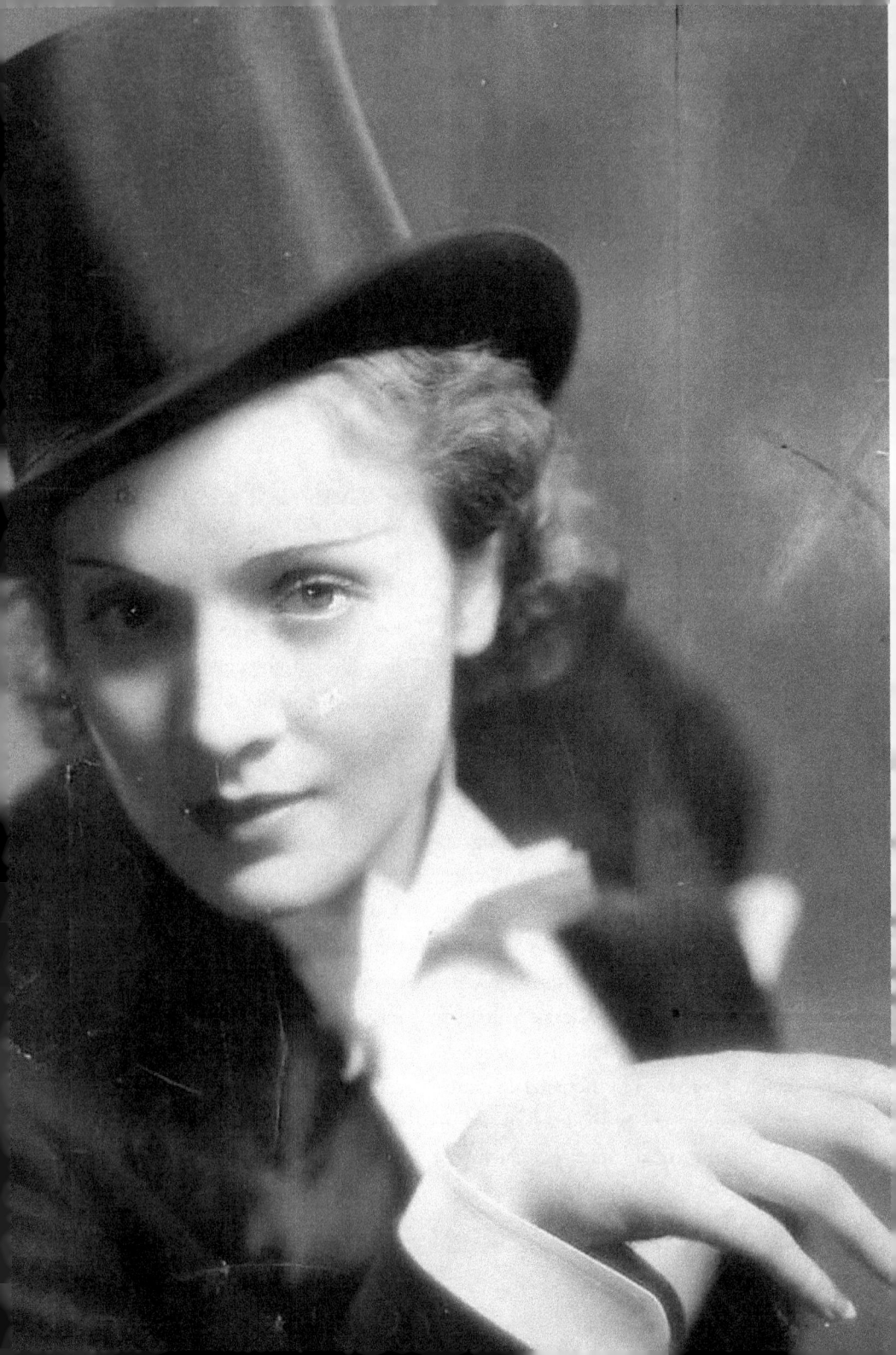

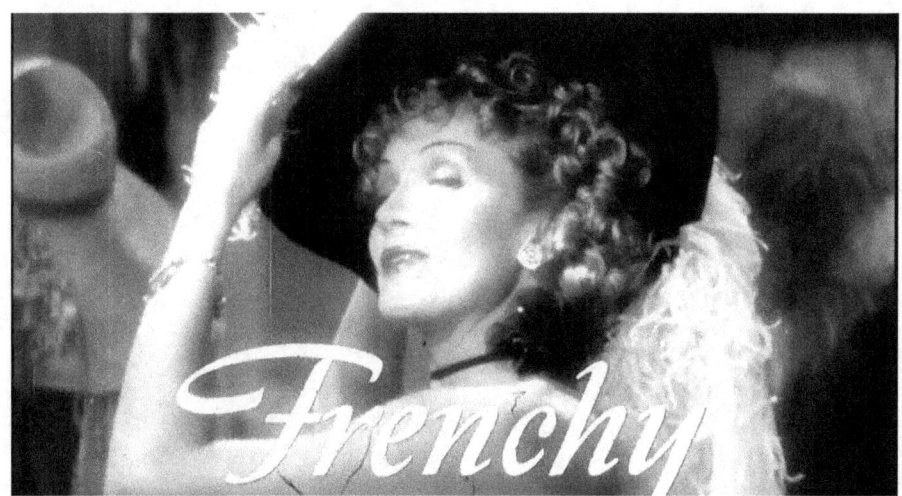

Frenchy

but for some reason the highly stylised Shanghai Express lingers longer in the mind.

It's well understood that Dietrich did her best work with von Sternberg, but even after they parted ways, she continued to hone her image on the screen, on the stage, and in life itself. Dietrich became larger than life, her name itself standing for something all together more meaningful. Dietrich meant glamour, bravery and defiance. Her last film with von Sternberg was The Devil is a Woman before she went her own way. She made Desire in 1936, a film she often called her personal favourite, or more to the point the only film she need not be ashamed of. There were commercial misfires, such as Angel (1937) for Paramount Pictures,

but she won the world over alongside James Stewart in Destry Rides Again (1939), a charming western with her at her comic best. Pure charisma, she stole the film from under Stewart's nose. Intentional or not, Marlene walked away with the picture.

Dietrich never enjoyed making movies, finding it tiresome and pressurising. Arguably her favourite role came during the Second World War when she devoted herself to entertaining the allied troops. Her work during the war, raising moral of soldiers, many injured and missing their home lives, with Dietrich touring and performing tirelessly, earned her the Medal of Freedom in 1947. Inevitably, anything that came after was bound to be a let down, and Dietrich soon tired of the movies,

appearing in less and less films as the years went on. Dietrich retained her glamour however. Famously bendable when it came to her sexuality, she was also an icon of modernism and style. Asked about her clothing, often controversial, she famously and defiantly replied, "I dress for the image. Not for myself, not for the public, not for fashion, not for men. If I dressed for myself I wouldn't bother at all. Clothes bore me. I'd wear jeans. I adore jeans. I get them in a public store – men's, of course; I can't wear women's trousers. But I dress for the profession."

The next phase in Dietrich's life, and certainly the part she seems to have enjoyed the most on a professional level, was her new life as a cabaret performer. From the fifties to the mid seventies when she retired, she toured the world singing songs and entertaining fans in every corner of the globe. Burt Bacharach has been her musical guide during the mid 1950s, and like she needed von Sternberg in the movies, she needed Bacharach when it came to the music. When Bacharach left to focus on song writing, she felt like she had lost her maestro. Yet on and on she continued, the illusion becoming more

carefully worked out as the years went by. Through delicate lighting, the right posture and costumes, not to mention the obligatory tape to pull back her face, the Dietrich myth moved on into new eras, never seeming to date or tire. It wasn't until bad health and pain forced her to quit that she retreated from the world's view. During a stage performance in 1975 she fell and broke her thigh, and with her legs being her two most valuable assets, she knew she only had one option.

She spent most of her final years in her Paris apartment, writing her memoir but refusing to see anyone but her daughter who helped care for her. Few pictures have been shown from the final seventeen years of her life, meaning that the aged, ailing Dietrich is a thing of the imagination and all we have are the films, the records, the stunning photographs, all featuring Dietrich in her prime. The myth is alive and well, but only because Marlene knew when to bow out.

Many people now know Dietrich for her personality, totally unaware of the enjoyable films. There are lost gems in there, like Witness to the Prosecution and Hitchcock's Stage Fright (1950), a

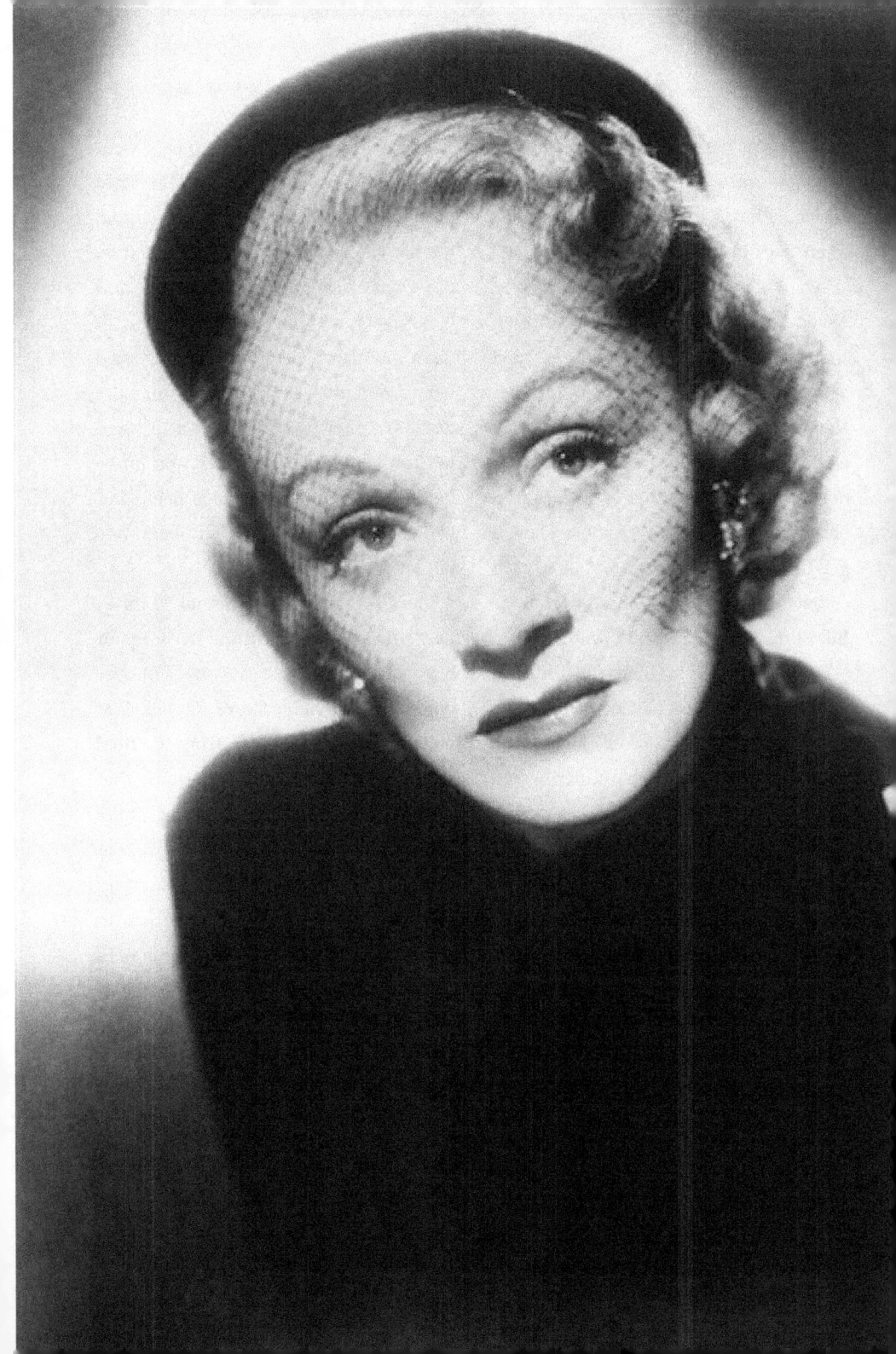

film which she walks away with, wonderfully playing a variation of her vampish image. It's all a very varied filmography for sure, starting in the pre-sound twenties in Europe and ending, poignantly, in the later 1970s with a cameo in David Hemmings' Just A Gigolo. These days, a person's fame too often takes precedence over the work that made them famous in the first place. I feel this has happened with Dietrich. Though Marlene was in many ways, and still is, an idea, a commodity, even a package - she was basically selling herself as the product - it's her films which we should really look to if we are to grasp the sheer size of her impact. Photographs may remain striking, audio recordings reminding us of her sensuous tones, but the films give us the larger than life Dietrich, in all her glory, preserved forever. While we may wonder what was so good about stars who existed before the advent of film, thankfully we have a filmography load of Dietrich delights to feast upon.

To say Dietrich's fame was just down to her films though, would be foolish. She was a myth in her own life time, and though she denied this, it was an enigma she created herself. "I am not a myth" she once famously said, though the fact she was addressing the issue suggests she knew she really was one. When Dietrich said those words, her career was definitely far from over. Her life in the movies was limited to a cameo now and then, but she was still a formidable and hugely popular entertainer, touring the globe with her singing act. She was still vital, performing at the age when most stars are retiring. For Marlene to admit she was mythical was to say she was but a face from the past, a nostalgic figure from Hollywood's bygone era. Now of course, with Dietrich gone, she really is a myth.

Dietrich was 90 at the time she died in 1992 of renal failure, and had been ailing for years, slowly crumbling away like rocks on a sea front. To Dietrich, the crashing waves were the world, the intrusive cameras of the press, the reaching hands of the people who loved her and yearned for one more glance. She kept the image alive until the end by concealing the inevitability of time, the sad reality of age. Forever a pro and a star to the end, she's forever Lil Marlene.

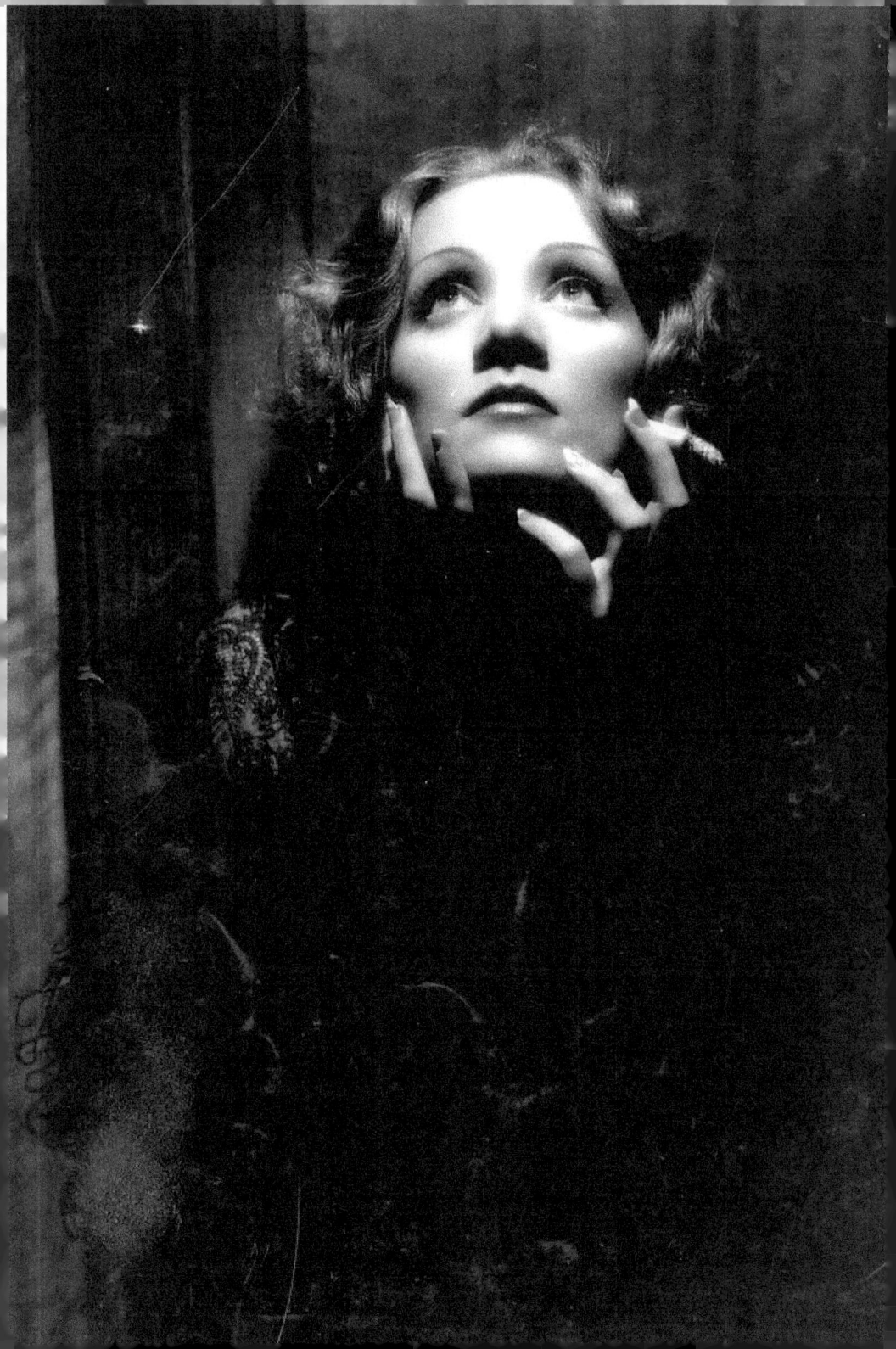

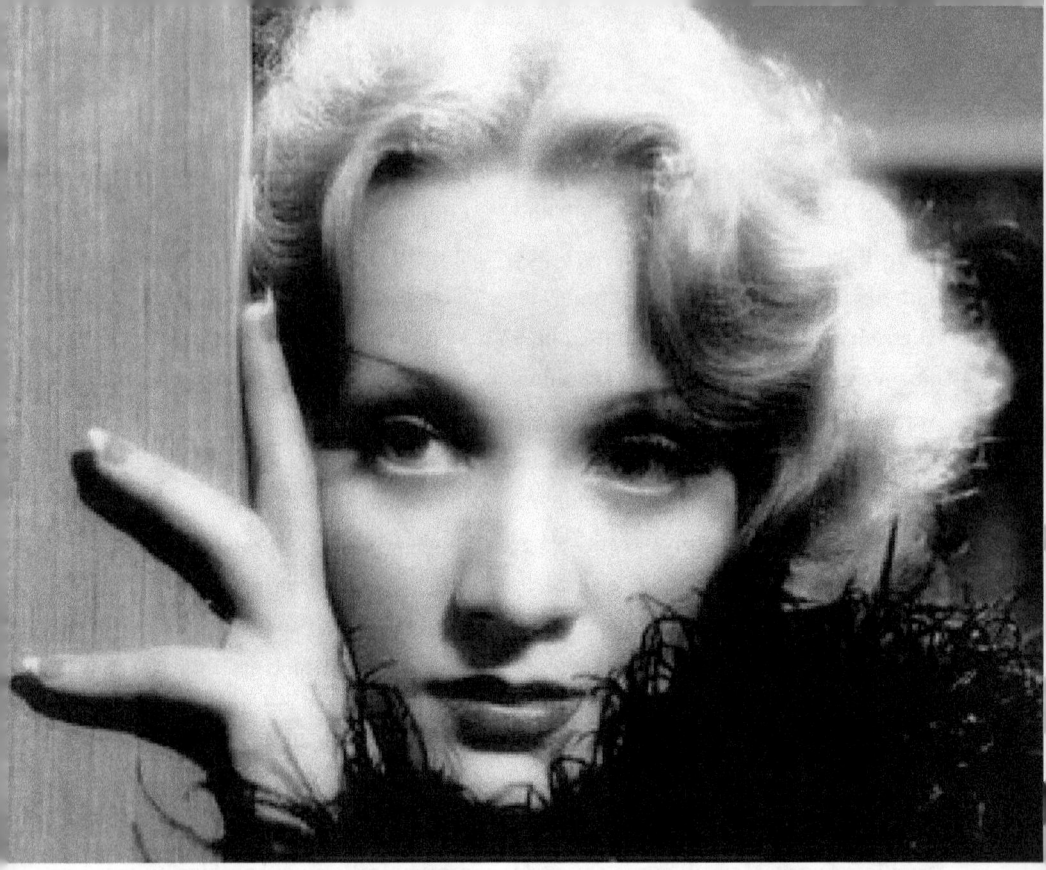

FILM SPOTLIGHT:

Shanghai Express

Dietrich As Fetish Glamour Icon

Shanghai Express is widely considered to be the pinnacle of Dietrich and von Sternberg's collaborations. Some of the other films they made together may be superior in other areas, yet in regards to presenting Dietrich as the perfect idol, a glamour icon completely out of reach to us mere mortals, Shanghai Express has no competition. It was also the biggest commercial success of the Dietrich and von Sternberg picture, making nearly 4 million at the time in the US alone. Clearly, an America suffering during the Great Depression found Dietrich and her immortal beauty a most satisfying distraction.

Shanghai Express is based on the story by Henry Harvey, concerning a train heading from Peking to Shanghai during the Chinese Civil War in 1931.

Clive Brook plays British Captain Donald Harvey, whose friends tell him he will be sharing the train with the famous Shanghai Lily, played by Dietrich, who actually turns out to be a former lover of his named Madeline, with whom he enjoyed a passionate affair long before she was known around the world under her new pseudonym. Their affair had ended five years earlier when a ploy set up by Lily resulted in him leaving her, but as is clear from their first meeting together, there are still feelings between the pair.

We are also introduced to other passengers on the express train, such as Lily's friend Hui Fei, played by the terrific Anna May Wong, eccentric English woman Mrs Haggerty (Louise Closser Hale in a dotty performance) and the strange, mistrustful Henry Chang, who is portrayed by Warner Oland.

A plot soon develops when the Chinese Government come on board in search of a rebel leader, and later on, thanks to Chang who sends a message out, the train is taken over by the rebel army, the leader of whom is Chang himself, who suddenly turns out to be a much more sinister character than we

first thought. Chang discovers that Captain Harvey is on his way to perform surgery on the Governor General of Shanghai, so needs him alive. Meanwhile Chang has his eyes on making Shanghai Lily his mistress, who uses his infatuation for her in a secret scheme to free the express train from the vicious rebels.

When written out the plot seems more exciting and engaging than it actually is in the film. The way von Sternberg paces the film and its thin storyline is rather unusual, in that the dialogue itself and the way it is delivered is flat, almost robotic in fact. The truth is that von Sternberg encouraged this mechanical way of speaking to emulate the rhythms of the train. It may make for slightly odd, disjointed viewing, but the voices and mannerisms do indeed blend in with the chugging grind of the engine. Acted in this way, the plot never feels sensational or unbelievable. Yes the film has a strangely surreal air to it, thanks to the performances, but there is no dramatic music, no flamboyant camera movements to enhance any of the action and there is never a sense of heightened excitement. Indeed, Shanghai Express is as steady and flat as

the grind of the train the characters are on board.

Paramount Pictures knew that a von Sternberg and Dietrich picture would always be costly, because costumes, lighting and sets had to look a certain way and von Sternberg himself had to take his time to achieve what he had set out to. They weren't always guaranteed hits of course (some of their other movies had been disappointments at the box office) but Paramount seemed happy enough to let the director indulge himself, as well as his most vivid fantasies. And let's face it, von Sternberg's most vivid fantasy, his wildest infatuation, his true obsession, was Marlene Dietrich herself.

This brings us to what is at the epicentre of this whole exercise in style and mood, Marlene, his goddess of glamour, whose very presence dominates the film. Everything that happens, every word, every line, every scene, every costume, every lavish set, and every set up is to lend gravitas to the arrival of Dietrich. When she's not on camera the viewer is thinking about when she will appear next, and when she's being filmed in all her glory we cannot take our eyes off her. If von

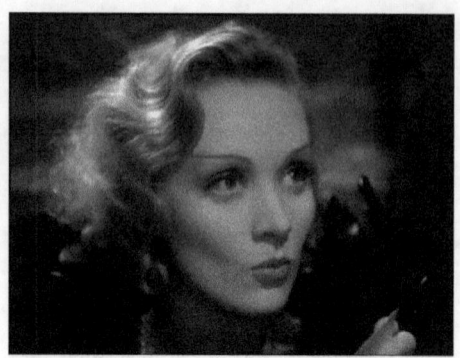

Sternberg's aim was to make a fetishistic item out of not just Dietrich herself but the very idea of her, then he succeeded.

Not so much as acting but more just being, Marlene is the embodiment of old style movie star charisma. Her exotic looks dazzle, her costumes hang on to her slender frame and her lines, often purred seductively, often spoken in that classic disjointed Dietrich manner, come forth like mini quotable nuggets, not realistic in any way, but highly memorable for that fact alone. When she isn't speaking, Dietrich is being a walking, or still-standing, work of art for the ever hungry von Sternberg, who seemed to get a thrill out of placing her in increasingly appealing circumstances and positions. Shanghai Express is a film yes, one with a plot that while easy to follow is still properly worked out, but for the most part this is movie not just as moving painting, but as showcase for

Dietrich. She is presented as a literal goddess throughout, put on a pedestal from her first appearance to her last.

It's worth noting that critics and admirers say it was Shanghai Express that made her a glamour icon and firm household name, and it's fair to say that it wasn't the film itself that enhanced her popularity but her appearance, or even more specifically her presentation, unveiled as she is like a great timeless masterpiece, within the picture itself. This was the fourth time von Sternberg and Dietrich had worked together, and by now he was an expert in Dietrich lighting. With Dietrich it was all about shadows, the spaces, where to place lights to accentuate her looks, her lips, her cheekbones, and perhaps most vitally of all, her legs. It might be wrong to call Dietrich's work in Shanghai Express a performance, for it is more of a reveal, an act of showmanship, a master class in effortlessly stealing scenes by just being present. Yes she was aided by a director who knew his star's best angles, and a brilliant cinematographer, Lee Games, who won an Academy Award for the film (Marlene later gave most of the credit to von Sternberg himself, who obviously guided the cinematography, given he knew his star so well), but Dietrich's self control and knowledge of her own power were vital factors in this glamour tour de force. The impact is also aided by tension. Dietrich's first appearance in the film is through a veil which covers half her face. As if to tease and titillate the viewer, von Sternberg does not reveal the enigmatic Dietrich until she is on board. Before then she is spoken of with excitement, a mythical character in her own life time. Once we are on board the train, Lily becomes the focal point for our senses, the plot secondary, and the other cast members standing by almost for the arrival of Dietrich's quietly towering presence. She does not need to try hard; she is effortlessly a star in every way.

Reviewers were impressed by the film upon its release, but most of all by Dietrich's star power. Many noted the control she had over her part and the audience. The New York Times praised her, writing, "Miss Dietrich gives an impressive performance. She is languorous but fearless as Lily. She glides through her scenes with heavy eyelids and puffing on her cigarettes. She measures every word and yet she is

not too slow in her foreign-accented speech. Clive Brooks's performance is also noteworthy, but he speaks in a monotone and is a little too hasty sometimes in his replies in conversations with Miss Dietrich."

Shanghai Express succeeds because it does not try to convince the viewer it is not a motion picture. This is escapism pure and simple, beautifully lit and photographed in seductive black and white, tasteful and assured in every scene, with all emphasis on the appeal of Dietrich. Josef von Sternberg became well known for his slow dissolves, which though began to tire some people a few pictures in, are handled masterfully here. The way the sequences blend together makes the transitions natural, often seamless, compared to the often jarring quality of some early sound pictures. And though one can fairly say that the delivery of the dialogue may put off modern viewers (there is, after all, almost a complete lack of emotion in the film), anyone with the patience to enjoy this film for what it is will be convinced that the technique works brilliantly. If anything, the disjointed speaking enhances the fact that we are in von Sternberg's alternative world, a place where myth and reality blend together to create a kind of enhanced dream state, emotionally stunted yet stylistically controlled.

Modern viewers attuned to fast moving plots, breakneck paces and snappily delivered dialogue may find Shanghai Express painfully old fashioned and slow. For others however, the film will come across as a soothing escape from modernity, a film which though fairly short feels endless in the best possible way. To compliment the film further, I would say that as soon as it finishes it would not be an odd choice to put it back on again, or to even have it showing in the background as you of about your day. There is a quality here that makes the movie a comforting pleasure, a treat. Shanghai Express is a classy, surrealistic distraction which may tread carefully through its flimsy plot, but does so with such grace that one wouldn't object to it being three hours long. The people and the words they speak blend wonderfully in with the visuals, as if being sucked into the hypnotism of the whole piece. We are in von Sternberg's fantasy now, and Dietrich is the queen of this hazy indulgence.

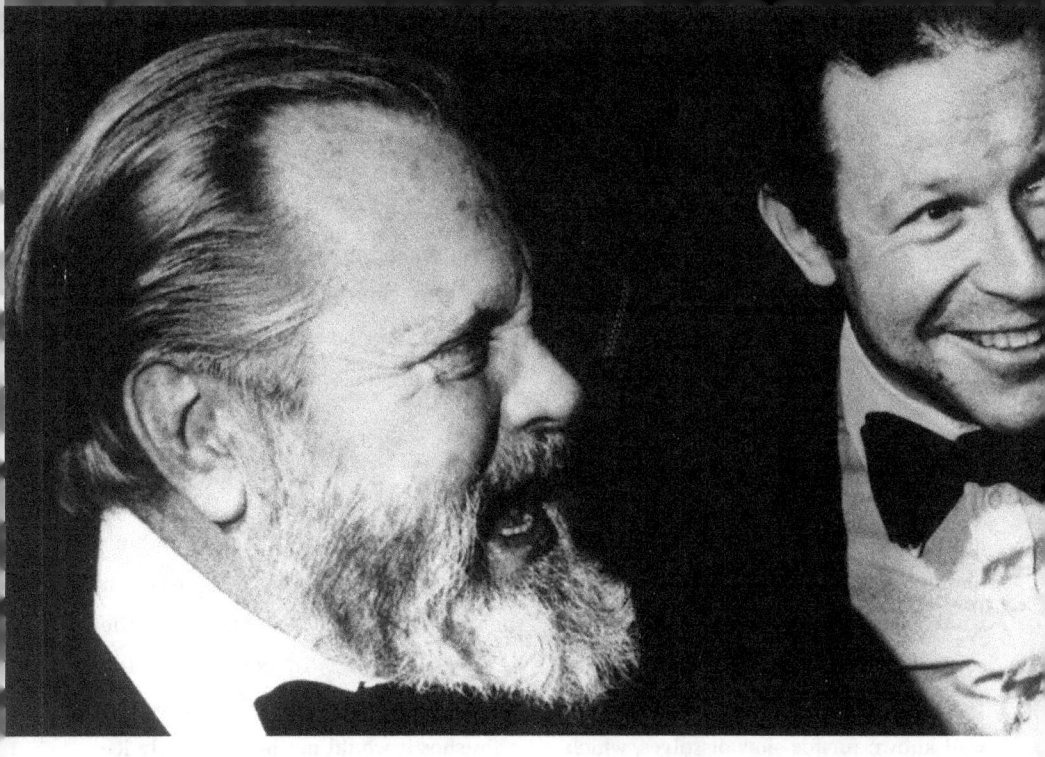

HENRY JAGLOM ON ORSON WELLES

I have spoken with the indie maverick filmmaker Henry Jaglom a few times over the past few years, and his stories never cease to amuse and entertain me. Jaglom was a former actor when he landed the job of editor on Easy Rider in 1969. With ambitions to become a filmmaker, he landed his first directorial job with 1971's A SAFE PLACE, a highly personal fantasy starring Orson Welles and Jack Nicholson. Befriending Welles later in the decade, his dinners with the legend are now preserved in the book My Lunches with Orson. Fittingly, Welles' final screen credit was with Jaglom in SOMEBODY TO LOVE. This

conversation, conducted in 2019, goes into Jaglom's experiences with Orson on and off set...

I am fascinated by the idea of you directing Orson, in your first film, A Safe Place. You said that he told you on the set that he realised you were making something different.

I will never forget that moment. It was after we did a scene with some animals in the zoo, trying to make an animal disappear. There was this elephant, it's on the outtakes if you've ever seen them. I remember after that scene, he said you're trying to do something really unusual here. I said am I? He said yes, it isn't conventional. I said no it's not. That turned his interest towards me more than anything else. That was the first thing that got him to pay attention. There was something about me that caught his attention. The second thing was, you probably know this, he asked me how filming was going and I said not well, because the crew were giving me a hard time. Do you know this story?

Yes I do, his advice to you about telling the crew it was all a dream sequence so they'd buy into it and do whatever you asked of them.

Oh you know it! You know all my stories! So those were the two memorable moments on A Safe Place.

So he saw you as a maverick, which he also was. He must have recognised that quality in you. Do you think that's why you went on to have such a deep friendship as the years went on?

Yes I would say so. I think that was why we ended up so close. We were both mavericks in a very different kind of way. But we each wanted to do our version of things as opposed to other people's ideas of how it should be done. He was drawn to me because of that. There is no question about that.

I wanted to ask about the book you released, My Lunches With Orson, the transcripts from your dinners together. You kindly sent me a copy and I have to say I love it. I must have read that book through ten times.

I think it really captured his personality.

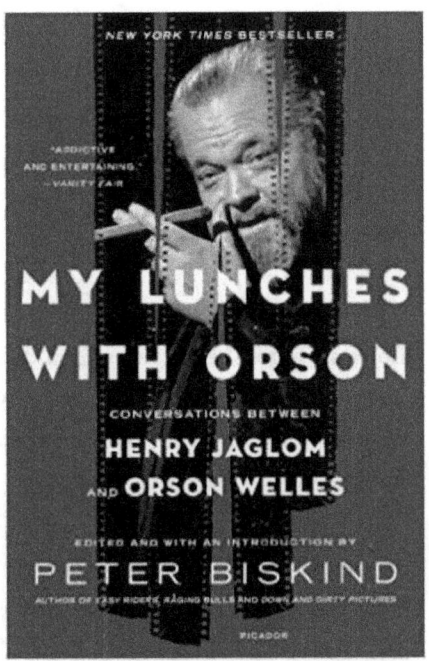

he particularly liked to stir me up. But Orson was a very progressive person all his life, politically. So he liked to play the part of the reactionary, telling me what a nice guy John Wayne was and all this stuff. But he was just being annoying and provocative. I am sure it was about the Sardinians having big thumbs, some ethnic nonsense. If you read the book you can tell there is a few times when he gets a kick out of annoying me. He liked to poke at my obvious reactions.

Yes I remember in the book at one point he says, I am more left than you will ever be, don't be so ridiculous.

Yeah. But at the same time when I got pissed off about these racist things he'd want to say what I had always known, that he had been very progressive. So why was he throwing me all these Irish things? It was really sort of bizarre, because it was not his personality at all. But he loved to stir things up and provoking a response. In my case he knew my politics, so he could come out and talk about his love for right wingers like John Wayne.

Me too. I love the way you are so honest with him about things, especially when he is being unreasonable, racist or bigoted. Do you think he liked the fact you had the balls to stand up and tell him when he was way off?

Oh of course. Of course he liked it. And he wasn't really racist, he was just playing the part, you know what I mean? He used to say those things to be provocative. You know the stuff about the Irish, or the Sardinians have fat thumbs, and all those stupid racist things. He knew that I would get crazy;

48

I think it's nice that your first film was with him and his last film, Someone to Love, was also directed by yourself. How had things changed in that period of fifteen or so years?

Oh it was all completely different. By then we were very good friends. That was his last year, a few months before he died when we shot that. I was editing it after he died; how long that was I am not sure. But yes, our relationship had totally changed. On A Safe Place I was just a kid who had convinced him to do it because he was playing a magician. I swear that is the only reason I got him to do the film.

Someone to Love is even more experimental in some ways though isn't it? I suppose he must have liked working on a different kind of thing because he was so used to doing voiceovers and commercials.

Well, he said, You know I have never been me on film. I have always put on a nose. I said, Well I have a good idea for a film and I want you to be in it. But I want you to be you, and he said, On no, not with this nose! I said, Orson you just

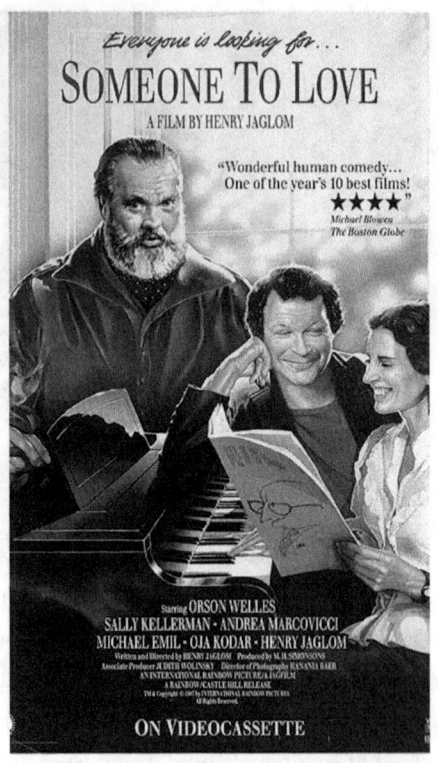

told me you'd be yourself. Eventually he said OK. And then he turns up for the first day of shooting and he's got on this weird kind of fake Roman nose and make up. I said Orson, what are you doing? The whole point of this was you were going to be yourself in the back of the theatre, talking about life and love and women. He said OK I will do that, but I can't do it with this tiny nose of mine. I said Orson, we discussed all this. So he said, OK you don't like this one, come back in an hour and I will have

49

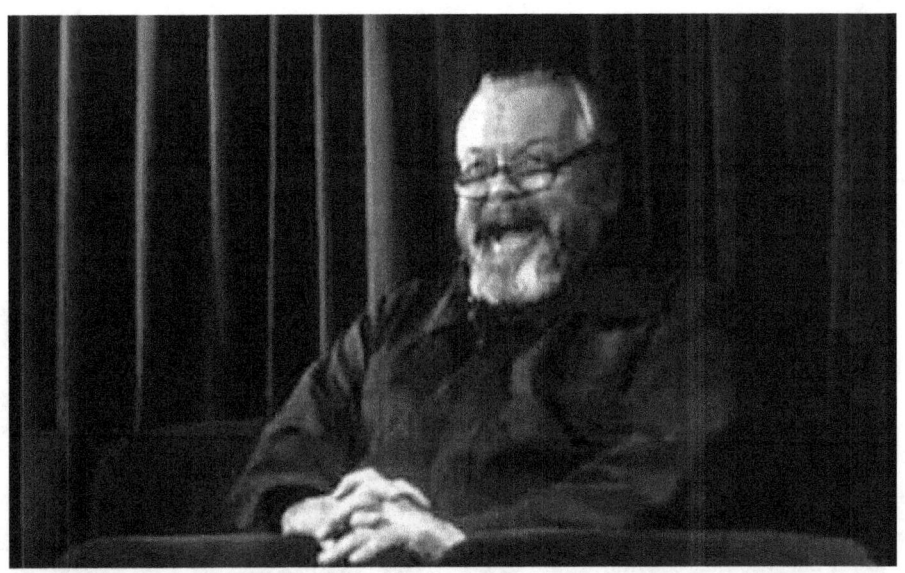

another. So I shot something and went back in an hour and he was dressed like an Arab. He had these strange eyes and everything, and another kind of nose, a kind of squared off nose. I said what are you doing? The whole point of this was to be yourself, with no make up or strange accents or anything. I think what it was, was that he was testing me, but he wanted me to trap him into it, and he was playing the part of someone being trapped into it, rather than admitting he was willing to do it. If he knew it was going to be his last performance on screen, he wanted it to be as himself. And it was also for the first time. And that was the wonderful thing about what we got in Someone to Love. For me it is very emotional, very moving, with him letting himself be himself before me. It was a great gift.

I wanted to ask you, what do you think Orson would think of his work getting all this recognition now?

Well he always said, When I die they are going to write books about me and they are going to be celebrating me. I can't get a penny now to make a movie, but they are going to romanticise me and put me into this category. It was infuriating for him, that even though he couldn't get a cent to make a new movie,

they would revere him in the end. He was very cynical about that. I remember once that he said that if he could just plunge into the future, after he was dead, he knew that he would get financing. But the trick would be how to bring that financing back while he was still alive. I remember that very well, it was very funny. I screamed at that when he told me. That was during a dinner we had. I remember that so clearly. It was New Year's Eve.

Well through the book, My Lunches with Orson, it's almost as if you are the last guy looking out for him. Did you feel like the last one, trying hard to get money and deals together for him?

Oh yeah, absolutely. I mean there is no question about that. Everyone I met wanted to have lunch with him but no one wanted to work with him or finance him. It was incredibly frustrating. At that point in time all my friends were the heads of the studios and producers and big movie stars, all of whom had been big fans of Orson when they were struggling. So I thought, Well now I can definitely get him financing. I thought they would all help, but it turned out none of them would help. It was disastrous. When I was trying to get a star to help finance The Other Side of the Wind (Orson's ongoing project, eventually released in 2018 by Netflix), no one would be in it.

That is what is so frustrating. Also, when he did get to film stuff, he was still great. The scenes he filmed later on were brilliant.

Absolutely. He never lost it at all. But it's all down to a very simple equation. None of his movies ever made any money so he couldn't get financing. He wasn't shocked by that, he was shocked by the fact that when he needed one of those seven big actors to help financing for The Other Side of the Wind, the actors all turned him down. That broke his heart. He said that actors had been ruined by money. Jack Nicholson really wanted to do it, but his agent said that all the work he had done to build up his career would collapse. Other producers would say, Why should we pay Jack all this money if he will do a film for a half a million dollars? It was shocking. But the whole film business got ruined that way.

51

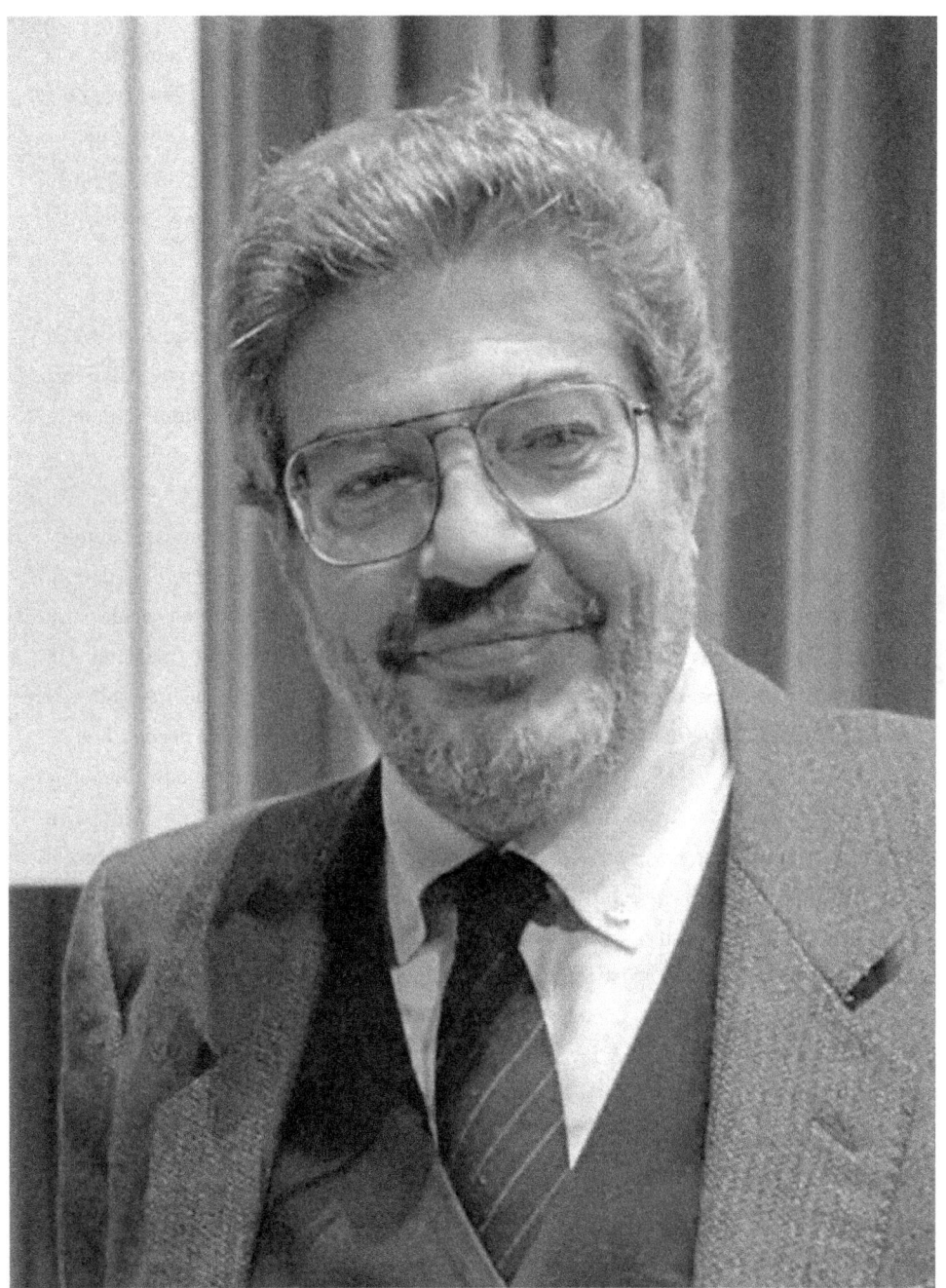

THE FILMS OF
ETTORE SCOLA

Ettore Scola was one of Italy's most celebrated and prolific filmmakers. Perhaps most remembered today for his seminal 1977 classic A Special Day, Scola's career was long and varied. Here, Chris Wade celebrates this icon of Italian cinema...

It's hard to define Ettore Scola's style as a filmmaker, artist and director in a manner which befits the man. While we can characterise fellow Italians Federico Fellini as the exuberant weaver of fantastical cinematic dreams, and Michelangelo Antonioni as the purveyor of modern alienation, Scola's films covered such a wide and varied area that it's impossible (and would even be misguided to try) to summarise his approach in one sentence. Concerned with social and political unrest, injustice and shifts, Scola approached society in all its shapes and forms, but he was more concerned, it could be said, with the individual within the society, whether it be the frustrated male, the put upon female, the expectant middle class father, the hopelessly poor or the hopelessly bourgeois. With his humour

intact at all times, Scola was a filmmaker concerned with humanity. But again, it is not as black and white as this.

Interviewed by the Cine Movel Foundation in 2009, Scola revealed his own views on the kinds of films he made, and vitally why he made them. "One could say that I've always done the same film, the themes are two or three. First of all there is time, which has fascinated me since I was young. The contemporary of time: chronological time flows away, but in actual facts we keep living experiences that have already occurred and that will happen again in the future. The important thing is the relationship between people and the facts that happen above them. I also like to work with another theme: history,

starting with the small events that are concerned with common people and their relationship with the bigger picture of history. This is the level that I am interested in... Decisions are being made somewhere else and stay in the background, what prevails is the history of humanity, the real and absolute history, that in which men are stronger than their dictators."

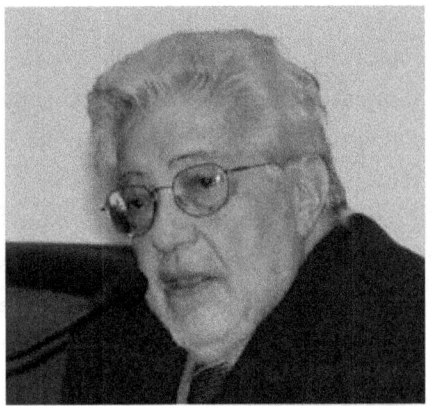

Indeed, Scola's intimate films of real people in real situations often act as microcosms for the bigger picture outside their small dichotomies. While Hitler and Mussolini are shaking hands in one of Scola's finest and best known pictures, 1977's A Special Day, Sophia Loren's frustrated housewife and Marcello Mastroianni's homosexual antifascist are experiencing something which may look inconsequential in comparison to the historic meeting of the two dictators, but is perhaps more emotionally captivating and more important on a directly humane level.

Scola's films were extremely varied, though what they all shared was an interest in human behaviour of all kinds. A look through his finest work reveals a consistency in drama with healthy doses of humour, and subtlety of varying degrees; his seminal 1974 breakthrough film We All Loved Each Other So Much about post-war readjustment; the grotesque comedy Ugly, Dirty and Bad (1976); the powerhouse drama A Special Day (1977); the witty and sophisticated That Night in Varennes (1982) about the ageing Casanova; Splendor (1989) about the slow death of in small town Italy as seen through the eyes of a theatre owner and his young projectionist; and What Time Is It? (1989), the tale of a father and son meeting up and facing their inner problems during a long day together. Scola was interested in human beings within a larger framework, and how changes affect individuals as well as the masses.

For Ettore Scola, cinema was not about entertainment, but communication and connecting human beings together

through a shared, common experience. "A film is a tale," he explained, "an irreplaceable means of communication, it corresponds to the written page but has a language which is accessible to everyone, in order to understand it one doesn't need the skills required to read Dickens. There isn't much awareness of the importance of cinema with reference to personal development and to its value as a political tool. TV has taken over because it allows to reach a very wide audience of electors. In any case, the large audience that sits in front of the telly is distracted and doesn't pick up too much from that, because the level of attention required by television is very different from that of cinema. The universal laugh that The Tramp can raise explains the role that cinema has had and can have, because cinema deals with themes that are intrinsic to human beings of all times and all continents."

Some of my favourite films of the past fifty years were directed by Scola. He began, like Fellini, as a cartoonist for the papers before becoming an anonymous gag writer in Italian comedies. He moved on to seeing his name on the screen writing credits before becoming a director himself. Though he had a shaky

start with some early lesser movies, he soon formed a style of his own, and a view that was as important, if not more so, than the contemporaries who seem to be much more celebrated than he does.

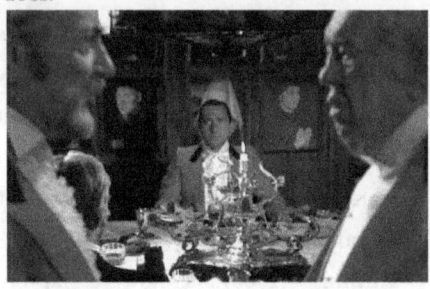

Ettore Scola's directorial debut came in 1964 when he had the opportunity to direct the great Vittorio Gassman in Let's Talk About Women, a broad comedy which though not as honed as his later dramatic work is a very funny and competent piece of work. Scola had already enjoyed a lot of experience as an anonymous writer then credited screenwriter, and his reputation was such that people were naturally a little disappointed with his first directorial outing. That said, Scola admitted that professionally it was a good first try, even if he did partly agree with the interviewer in the 2016 documentary on his career when he referred to the film as crap. Let's Talk About Women is a

likeable comedy, but by no means is it among Scola's finest work.

Scola continued to make broad, light comedies into the mid sixties, Hard Time for Princes being released in 1965. Also starring Vittorio Gassman, paired as unlikely as it seems with Joan Collins herself, the film is all but forgotten now and rarely if ever gets singled out when Scola's work is discussed. One can understand why, for it is certainly one of his weakest films.

Thrilling (1966) is now a largely overlooked entry in the Italian anthology genre. It consists of three tales, directed by Scola, Carlo Lizaani and Gian Luigi Polidoro respectively. All the finest anthology films, whether from the fifties or sixties, had a loose theme tying them together (from Boccaccio 70 to Spirits of the Dead, the former consisting of four broad comedies, the latter all based on tales by Edgar Allen Poe), and Thrilling's form is in the fact that all three stories are based on ordinary men who take to crime. Scola's segment, first up in the picture, is Il vittimista. It concerns Nino Manfredi as a complacent, arrogant teacher who actually lives under the tyrannical ruling of his wife, played by Alexandra

Stewart, is smoothly done, with nice performances and a decent musical score (by Ennio Morricone no less), but Scola's addition is outshone by Carlo Lizzani's L'autostrada del sole, starring Alberto Sordi and Sylva Koscina.

After his rather muted short in the anthology film Thrilling, he went from one genre piece to another, the crime film to the fantasy comedy. The Devil in Love (1968), featuring once again Vittorio Gassman, here alongside, rum as it is, Hollywood veteran Mickey Rooney, is a rather silly but sometimes admittedly funny romp.

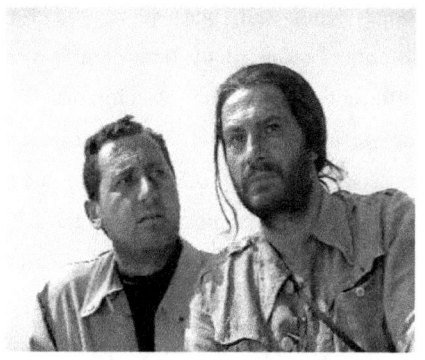

Scola's next film is what many consider to be his first important piece of work, the hilariously titled Will Our Heroes Be Able to Find Their Friend Who Has Mysteriously Disappeared in Africa? Scola first started work on it as far back as 1965, in the midst of making

his early broad comedies, but it was not completed until 1968. Scripted by Scola himself with Agenore Incrocci and Furio Scarpelli, it is the start of his serious filmography.

It follows Fuasto Di Salvio, a businessman bored of his life who decides to flee the mundanity of his existence and go to Africa after receiving the news of his brother in law's death out there. With his employee Ubaldo, Fausto travels to Angola and begins his journey, heading in the footprints of the deceased man. When he proves impossible to find, though his legend looms large in the area, Fausto and his friend are captured by natives, the leader of whom is a most unexpected person indeed.

Though the films that preceded it were often enjoyable and had their merits, this is the first time Scola made a film which went beyond the limitations of broad Italian comedy. Wonderfully acted by a cast including Alberto Sordi and Nino Manfredi, it's beautifully directed by Scola who, in a tricky location, manages to capture some stunning sights and shoot genuinely exciting sequences while still ensuring the plot, which becomes increasingly

surprising, sees itself out to a well balanced conclusion. Scola proved here that those early films had been good experience, practise if you like, to take on a difficult film such as this.

Speaking of shooting on location for the film, Scola said: "In actual facts I never started out with the location, the inspiration came from reading Salgari, Verne and Conrad as a young boy. Since those were wealthy times for cinema, we made surveys according to the subject, then we wrote the script, so I travelled in Africa from Kenya to South Africa and Chad. In Angola I found what I was after: a setting in evolution..."

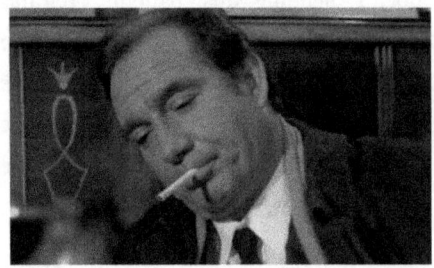

Scola's next feature saw a drastic change in style and setting, 1968's Police Chief Pepe. Working with another true Italian great, the wonderful Ugo Tognazi, Scola's Police Chief Pepe is a risque comic drama. Ugo plays Antonio Pepe, an Inspector in a small Northern Italian city who uncovers and

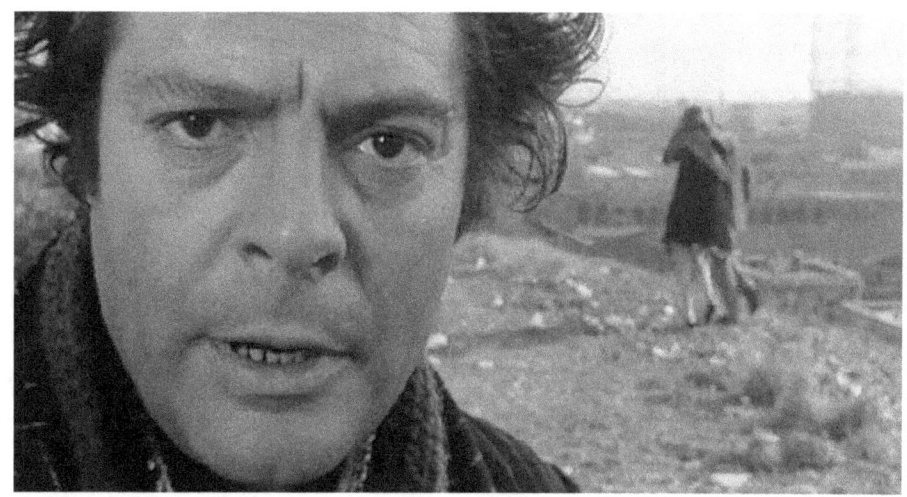

investigates a prostitution ring run by a pair of old age pensioners. Along the way he uncovers much seediness in the streets, including an overly watchful headmaster who ogles the pupils, a doctor bedding his patients, regular orgies staged by a well known noblewoman and worst of all the fact his girlfriend poses for pornographic magazines. Pepe wishes to uncover the sin that pollutes this so called pure city, but the powers that be push against him.

This is both one of Scola's finest earlier pictures and also one of his most obscure. Now more widely known for Armando Trovajoli's rich score, it's a no holds barred expose of society's under belly, with Scola tearing through every level of so called respectability. A true social satire, it's held together by a solid performance from Tognazi, but again, it's Scola's ironic observations and no frills direction which brings the film together. Though some may sniff at Scola's moralistic position (he never judges but continuously points out), Police Chief Pepe is a bold, brave film that was way ahead of its time.

Marcello Mastroianni had been one of the biggest icons of world cinema in the 1960s, appearing in some of the most memorable - now legendary - movies of the time. While being seen overseas as the world's greatest Latin Lover (an image he hated), he quickly established the fact he was one of the most versatile and talented actors around. He started his new decade as a mega star with Ettore Scola, in the first of their many collaborations. Of all Mastroianni's films

form the decade, The Pizza Triangle (1970) - scripted by Scola and writing team Age and Scarpelli - is a particular stand out which has a healthy reputation in the history of Italian cinema. The film follows Antonioni's leading lady Monica Vitti as Adelaide, a florist dating Orese (Mastroianni), a married man in his own right, who sees their relationship invaded by the arrival of pizza cook Nello (Giancarlo Giannini). The threesome decides to live together, but this unlikely situation invites more stress and trouble, resulting in a tragic finale that may jar with the light comedic tone of the rest of the film, but delivers a punch nonetheless.

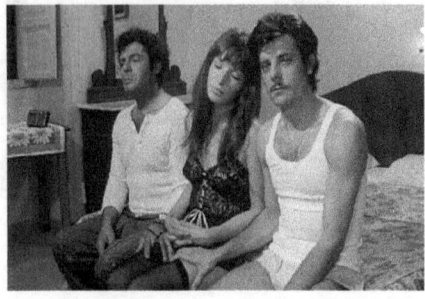

The Pizza Triangle is the start of a run of fine performances Marcello gave in Ettore Scola films, this one winning him a Cannes Best Actor Award. Speaking years later, Mastroianni remembered it as a good film but was curious what he did in this film and didn't do in others that warranted a Canes Best Actor gong.

Scola and Mastroianni made for a strong duo, and in their work they highlighted the injustices, absurdities and dark ironies of society and everyday life. The Pizza Triangle has their humour turned up to the maximum, though the dark twist gives it a stranger aura than most broad Italian comedies of the era. Prior to this, Gassman had been undoubtedly the screen alter ego of Scola, a man who could perfectly make his way through the absurdities of Scola's vision of Italy. Here, with Mastroianni, he came across an actor with whom he could take on any subject, not just limited to the Italian comedy, as would be proven by their later collaborations. As gifted at comedy as at drama, Mastroianni became the premier male of Scola's unique brand of cinema. This is a wild, feral, often electrifying display of acting, certainly one of Marcello's best from this era, regardless of his own thoughts on his performance.

Mastroianni did however consistently claim it to be one of the finest films he ever made. "The Pizza Triangle is a film I am very attached to," he said in the nineties, "for me, it is a real masterpiece.

A return to working class characters who were at the same time transformed by a new kind of language in a more fantastical atmosphere which was highlighted by an interesting ironic vein. I had a lot of fun playing this ingenuous, retarded communist..."

It is, of course, a class comedy, and Scola, Age and Scarpelli fearlessly take on the political climate of Italy during that period, Communistic misunderstandings, class restrictions and the modern city, littered with trash and oozing out consumerist blood from its painful sores. Also released as Jealousy Italian Style, the film is not easy to track down commercially in English; which is a shame, as most of Marcello's other films with Ettore - such as Splendor, What Time Is It? and A Special Day - are readily available on DVD. This is a buried gem that deserves more credit and should get a wider release.

Only a year after his first film with Marcello Mastroianni, Ettore Scola teamed with the Italian icon once again for My Name is Rocco Papaleo. From s screenplay by Scola, Peter Goldfarb and Ruggero Maccari, My Name is Rocco Papaleo stars Marcello as Rocco, an Alaskan who ends up in Chicago going

through a series of increasingly bizarre situations. Though the journey begins with the wide eyed innocent enjoying his trip, it winds up with the corruptive nature of America destroying his simplicity.

The film often feels a little messy, at least in comparison to their previous film (and indeed the gems to follow) but the point about the dark power of America is hammered home so well that one doesn't mind. Marcello, never one to disappoint, gives another solid characterisation, expertly documenting this man's decline from happy go lucky soul to defeated husk.

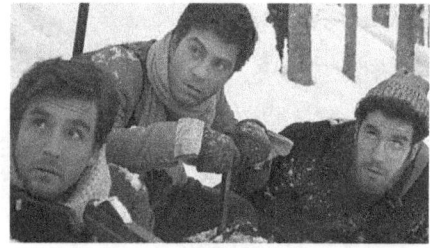

1972 saw the release of The Most Wonderful Evening Of My Life, a French-Italian comedy drama produced by Dino De Laurentiis and based on the novel A Dangerous Game by Fredrich Durrematt. Scola also directed other important works in this period, such as We All Loved Each Other so Much. For some time it was considered an essential

Italian film of the post-pink realist era, and only now does it seem to be getting less praise.

Once in a while a film comes along which is just perfect, works in all the right ways and delivers its message with a directness so brave that it makes you wonder how more filmmakers don't end up achieving such greatness more often. A Special Day (1977) is such a film, a quietly magical experience which gets by on a sharp script, controlled direction, a message which still packs a punch and two excellent performances by two all time greats, arguably at their best as dramatic performers, even though they had already scaled the heights of their profession.

A Special Day is special in itself because it brings back together Marcello Mastroianni and Sophia Loren. In this scenario they are starring as two atypical types in another gem produced by Loren's husband, Carlo Ponti. The special day in question is certainly one of the most memorable in Italian history; the 6th of May, 1938, the day Adolf Hitler visited Rome to meet with Mussolini. Loren plays a down to earth homemaker, Antonietta, who from the first second of the film proves that with her six kids and arrogant husband has a little too much on her plate to even have a second to herself. On the day in question, she stays at home while her family, including her husband Emanuele who is a full on fascist in his political beliefs, join in a street parade to greet Adolf.

After the opening whirlwind scene, with the camera endlessly floating round the hustle and bustle of the family home, the constant activity with which Antonietta must struggle, the tired out mother is left alone. Nodding off for a second, she listens to the parade on the radio as the day unfolds. While feeding the family's pet bird, she turns around to get it some food only for it to fly out of a window and escape. She believes the whole block is out, save the moustached female caretaker, and then realises that her charming neighbour Gabriele (Marcello) has also stayed in. Seeing the bird is near his window, she goes round and the pair, him reluctant at first, scramble around and eventually retrieve the bird. As the day goes on, Gabrielle visits her home and the pair bond over coffee. When the caretaker informs her that Gabriele is a traitor to fascism, Antonietta loses interest and

discourages any further developments in their friendship. His anti fascist stance is also made clear when he cynically goes through her scrap book of Mussolini, picking out quotes which highlight Mussolini's backward view of society and women in particular. One quote sticks in his throat, that for a man to be a real man he must be a husband, a father and a soldier. Though the viewer is beginning to get the fact, subtly, that Marcello's character is a homosexual, Antonietta is oblivious to his sexuality and is charmed by him.

When she does learn of his sexuality, she has none of it, though clearly hurt by her attitude, Gabriele confronts Antonietta about her rigid attitudes and expectations of men. On the roof, where they have just been folding up the washing, he mocks her beliefs that a real man has to think with his genitals, manhandling her in a mocking fashion. Antonietta runs back to her room, warning Gabriele that his shouting will alert the caretaker. But Gabriele, who at the start of the film was about to shoot himself, doesn't care what the caretaker over hears. Near the beginning of the film when talking on the phone to someone, he admits that he could grab the next person and tell them everything about his life. This desperation is evident in the stairwell as she shouts loud and proud to the caretaker. In her eyes he is a fascist sinner, a dirty homosexual who denies the purity of their fascist leader. Guilty, Antonietta goes to Gabriele's flat where he is making eggs, and as if to make peace, the pair dine quietly together. Eventually, Antonietta admits she has quickly developed a crush on him, and in a tender moment the pair make love on a bed. For him, it is a pleasant distraction from the doom that lay ahead for him; for her it is a deep meeting between two bodies, two souls, an experience she has never gone through in her life, especially not with her boorish husband. Gabriele, though admitting it was pleasant, regretfully informs her that it will change nothing of his sexuality, though he says he is glad he met her and they had their moment, especially on this most symbolic of days.

The day goes on and the people begin returning from the rally. When the family arrives home, the children are excited about having seen the two dictators together, marking it as a

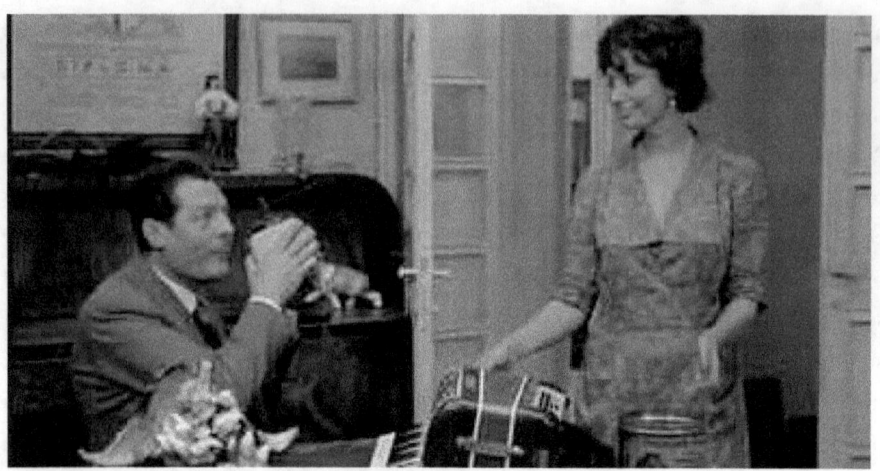

landmark day in history they were lucky enough to witness. Antonietta however, remains miles away at the kitchen table, present in body but absent in mind, her thoughts on Gabriele. As night comes, the family all go to bed and her husband, besotted with the fuehrer, wishes to conceive their seventh child that night, naturally to be named Adolfo.

With the kids tucked up in bed and husband waiting for his wife to join him under the sheets for a quick bed spring symphony, Antonietta sits by the window, reading the Musketeers novel Gabriele gave her as a gift. With a sadness and emptiness behind the eyes, she watches Gabriele leave his apartment, accompanied by two men who are taking him to a boat where he will be deported. The light of his apartment goes out and Antonietta sees him descend the stairs. Slowly, she gets up, turns out the lights and heads for her bedroom, removing her dress and turning off the bedside lamp.

Ettore said of his film: "From childhood, history was a subject that fascinated me, and what I kept wondering was how everyday life might have been different, if Caesar or Mussolini had changed course. My sympathy always went to those millions who didn't participate in those choices, but had to follow them."

A Special Day uses Antonietta's predicament and general situation as a microcosm of Italian life under fascism, and the female's place in such an

antiquated and harsh society. Loren, always at her best when playing a normal Italian woman, is excellent as Antonietta, a woman of her time unable to break the norm and the plight of her constricting situation. She puts on a brave face, her scrap book of Mussolini a symbol for her compromise and submission into a life which offers her nothing emotionally and drains her physically.

Marcello's Gabriele offers Antonietta an alternative to her prison, temporarily freeing her from the cell in which she has found herself and opening a window into sensuality, the beauty of connection and the alternative to the fascistic attitude. Marcello embodies the liberal minded side of his nation, playing against type but doing so wonderfully. From the word go, this is a beautifully observed, finely nuanced performance. In his first scene, after Antonietta sees him from the back at his desk, he toys with the gun in a way that suggests to us with silence he is contemplating suicide. When Antonietta knocks on his door he fussily rearranges and tidies his desk in a way her insensitive husband never would. Even such a tiny detail offers a clue about Marcello's sexuality and tenderness, his sensitivity and vulnerability. When asked by Duck Cavett how he achieved such gentle delicacies, which perfectly summed up his character, Marcello said it was simply a case of observing his gay friends, getting physical clues and storing them for later. He also spoke of how sickening it was in fascist Italy that homosexuality was condemned, which suggests that his own personal views on the issue leaked into his authentic performance. Indeed, there is one scene in particular when Gabriele's emotions become too much. He shouts down to the caretaker, "let her know that I'm a queer", he yells, reeling off derogatory slang terms for a homosexual, like faggot and bender. There is a look in his eyes that suggests a man tortured by the rigidity of the establishment, its misguided hatred based on sexuality. In his voice, quivering in rage, and movements verging on wild, careless hysteria, one can see Gabriele yearns to live in a land where he is accepted for himself, where he can feel free and be embraced. It's a wonderfully enlightening moment in a performance which can only be called masterful. It is also profoundly moving.

The careful considerations he applies in the role remind the viewer what a vast range Mastroianni had, both emotionally and character-wise. Earlier in the seventies he had played the ultimate womanising bastard in La Grande Bouffe, perfectly believable as a heartless lothario on the quest for physical gratification with no regard for the feelings of others. In Fellini's twin masterpieces, La Dolce Vita and 8 1/2, he came across as a detached witness to the disorder of modern life, disconnected from a reality that was dream like but emotionally alienating. Here, he was as tender as could be, a man who understood the plight of the female in a fascist dictatorship and lived life as an outsider, sacked for his sexuality and eventually deported from a country that did not want his kind amongst them.

While Vittorio De Sica had brought out the fun, dynamism and life of the Loren and Mastroianni pairing, Italian great Ettore Scola brought out the true humanity. Removing Loren of all glamour and Marcello of all machismo, he reveals the depth of both actors who play their roles so well it's impossible, quite literally, to imagine anyone else in their place. The script by Ettore, Maurizio Costanzo and Ruggero Maccari gives the leads plenty of room to flesh out their parts, enhance them from potential stereotypes or archetypes at best and into fully formed, multifaceted people full of complexities. Marcello being gay and anti fascist alone may have been too broad a reactionary point against the system had it not been for his restrained, finely tuned efforts, what Ettore often called his rare simplicity. As powerful as the actors are, it is the eye of Ettore that ensures the drama remains real and gripping. In the early scenes he floats around the tired out mother restlessly, floating with her through rooms to highlight her fatigue amidst this repetitive boredom of her daily existence. In the more up front moments however we can almost feel the heat of the one way passion, the wet in Loren's eyes and the indifference in Mastroianni's, so painfully close it almost hurts. Not a second is wasted in this remarkable two hander, which is in my view one of the most straight forward, un-sensational and yet relentlessly enthralling films of its time.

Reviews were glowing, with most critics celebrating the latest from Sophia and Marcello, arguably world cinema's

most likeable on screen duo. The New York Times loved it, raving, "In Ettore Scola's funny, humane A Special Day — an acting tour de force for Sophia Loren and Marcello Mastroianni — Antonietta and Gabriele are never really a couple, but their brief encounter lights up the screen with the kind of radiance you get only from great movie actors who also are great stars. It's something, I suspect, that only Miss Loren and Mr. Mastroianni could bring off so triumphantly. A Very Special Day is pure theatrical contrivance, and this is part of the pleasure as we watch two extraordinary performers test themselves, take risks, find unexpected pockets of humour and pathos in characters that one doesn't easily associate with the public personality. Miss Loren is magnificent in the best role she's had since Two Women, for which she won an Academy Award."

Loren herself was at first reluctant to take on the role, it being unlike any other she had played before. During the first week of filming she was not having a good time, reportedly miserable on set despite her old friend Marcello's presence, simply because the director would not allow her usual trusty make up artists and assistants anywhere near her. Thankfully however, she soon accepted the way things were and got on with her job.

Speaking to Interview Magazine upon release, Loren said of the film, "When we decided to do something together, Scola was a little worried because he wanted to top, if he could, whatever Marcello and I had done with De Sica. He wanted a new way to show us on the screen with new faces, in new situations. Then he came with an approach, which my husband and I thought was the right one and the story came out beautifully. Of course, it's a very courageous story to do because nowadays you see... films that exalt violence and erotic films and there is none of that in the film."

Into the 1980s Scola continued to make grounded but engaging movies, such as 1980's The Terrace. He joined forces with Mastroianni once again for 1982's That Night At Varennes, a long, winding tale set in 1791 about a group of well-to-do rich folk who get caught up in the French revolution while all travelling cross country in a stagecoach together. At nearly three hours, Scola manages to keep the film interesting with imaginative direction and camera

shots which bring us intimately among the bright and vibrant, though often painfully flawed, characters.

The script is lively and full of little nuggets (it was the last screenplay of veteran Sergio Amidei before he died), but it is the cast that ensure this movie remains engaging. Mastroianni is

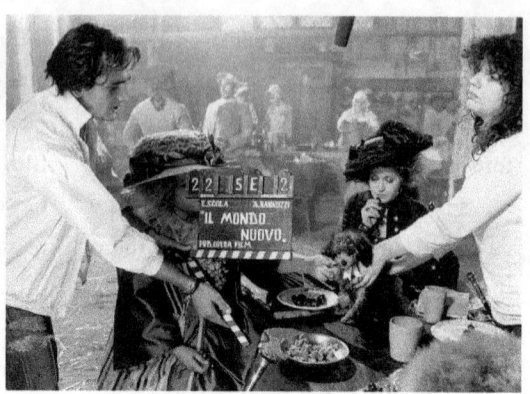

masterful as an ageing Casanova, a man whose womanising reputation precedes him. But this is not the young, virile ladies' man of legend; Marcello's version is more jaded, more tired, yet still as vain as ever. There is one marvellous scene where he removes his wig in a rest room and we see his few remaining strands of hair, wildly blowing in all directions. As good as the rest of the cast are - Harvey Keitel, Hanna Schygulla and Jean Claude Brialy all stand out - Marcello's work is towering here and he quietly, without having to do very much quite often, dominates the film.

Any film buff will know that Fellini's Casanova was only a few years old at this point. Donald Sutherland has embodied Fellini's image of the lover, a tormented, loathsome, fiendish character trying to feed a hunger that could never be truly fed. Marcello's Casanova is more exhausted, no longer worried about fulfilling his legend and living up to expectations. He is a shadow of the infamous myth, yet those around him still hold him in awe. Scola's vision of Casanova is more realistic and, it has to be said, much more effective.

The New York Times found it an admirable feat, writing, "The small talk here is never small. But it is wonderfully casual at some times, quietly resonant at others, and always exquisitely delivered. If La Nuit de Varennes offered nothing more than the ensemble acting on display, it would be major and memorable on that basis alone." They also added, and quite rightly too, "Of all the fine performances here, Mr. Mastroianni's is the most dazzling, because he plays the vainest of men without bringing any of his own vanity

to the role. This Casanova is on his last legs, rueful about the ways in which his body now disappoints him and yet forever interrupting conversations to powder his nose. He's also a wonderfully gallant figure, and never one of whom the film makes fun…"

Scola's direction was also singled out for its reluctance to go overly elegant. Though his vision is one of grace, he keeps these characters as real people, not distant figures of sophistication.

Still, Roger Ebert was not overly impressed, complaining in his review "With such a promising premise, director Ettore Scola can hardly go wrong. But he does, in a long, rambling movie that contains moments of great charm, a couple of wonderful performances, and a great deal of self-indulgent tedium. The movie takes the basic situation of John Ford's "Stagecoach" (and countless other movies) and loads it with so many mannerisms, asides and nice little directorial flourishes that we finally lose patience."

La Nuit de Varennes has a good reputation in world cinema, and remains one of Scola's most acclaimed works. It was screened at Cannes in 1982 and also received a nomination from the National Board of Review of Motion Pictures. That said, by no means is the film a good starting point for Scola newcomers, though Mastroianni's painfully human performance does offer the viewer a way into this wordy, very long and what may be to some an often challenging film.

This said, Ettore Scola was incapable of making a bad film it seems, and with whatever subject matter he took on, he always injected it with the right amount of drama, humour and pathos. In 1985's Macaroni, he was gifted with the presence of two legendary actors, Marcello Mastroianni once again, and American icon Jack Lemmon. The trio of Scola, Mastroianni and Lemmon promised to be a memorable meeting of minds, and as one might expect, the results of their collaboration were extremely memorable.

Macaroni concerns Lemmon as Robert Traven, the head of a large company who is in Naples on business. Tired, stressed out and lost in the mist of meetings and corporate nonsense, he is a man whose best and happiest years are behind him. He is in the midst of a divorce, and though making a lot of

money he lives a joyless existence. When getting to his hotel one evening, there is a knock on the door. Standing there is Antonio (Marcello Mastroianni), a man who claims to be an old friend from the 40s. As is revealed by a photo he hands over, Robert used to date his sister Maria at the back end of the Second World War. Yet Robert has no recollection, at least not at first, and the two men part on bad terms, Robert even giving Antonio the finger as he leaves for the elevator.

However, the photo has piqued his curiosity, and the next day he is driven to Antonio's work place to hand over the photo. He asks him to keep it, and ever more curious about this mysterious Maria he barely remembers, Antonio and Robert end up spending the day together. They visit Maria, now married, a grandmother set up in a grand home. Bizarrely, Robert has become a mythical god-like figure to her and her family, mainly because Antonio has been consistently writing letters claiming to be from Robert, recounting his various made-up and often very far fetched adventures across the world. Antonio did it at first to spare his sister's feelings, hurt as she was by the sudden absence of

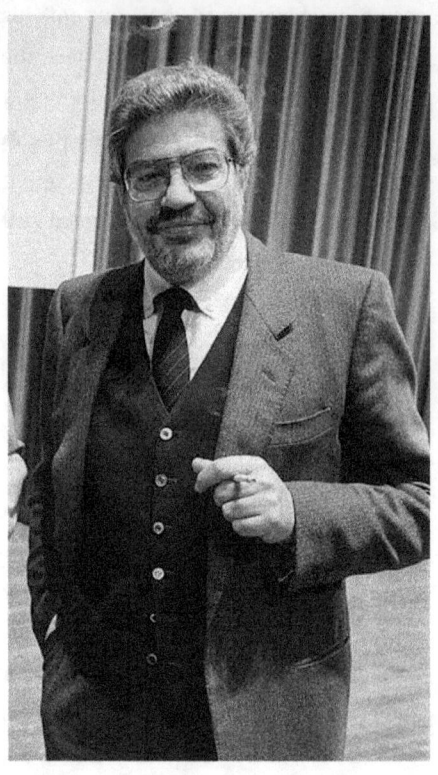

her American lover, but soon began to enjoy writing them so much he kept it up for forty years. A frustrated writer himself, Antonio gets out his literary aspirations in the letters, but later admits it wasn't really Robert who was experiencing these fantasies through the letters, but Antonio himself.

The relationship between the two men continues to grow, and develops further as it is revealed Antonio's son has got muddled up with gangsters over a

money issue. After a show down with the gangsters, where an excited Robert seems to have lived out one of his fantastical scenarios from the letters, the two men sit by the harbour to enjoy a bagel. I will not reveal the finale just in case any viewers do not want it spoiling for them, but it is most unexpected and very moving indeed.

Macaroni is a little slice of irresistible film magic, a lovely film boasting two wonderful, energetic performances. It's a thrill to see the uptight Lemmon slowly unravel and become a man learning to love life again, and he performs it with his usual believability. Marcello is wonderful as the affable Italian, leading his guest by the arm around the various wonderful sights in Naples. As his own inner complexities come to the fore, Marcello's part deepens and his portrayal of Antonio stands up as one of his best from the 1980s.

Written by Scola himself with the help of Ruggero Maccari and Furio Scarpelli, Macaroni has a sharp, funny and often poignant script. Some may see it as a criticism of American capitalism, of greed and the thirst for money, but Scola does not elevate Italian life above any other. Lemon's character merely stands for the business class while Mastroianni, who just happens to be Italian, sees life from a more grounded outlook. There is some rich and quotable dialogue ("It's beautiful to waste time") and there are turns in the plot which are genuinely surprising. It is perhaps one of Scola's most engaging films. Like A Special Day, it concerns two very different people coming together and experiencing something extraordinary. The homosexual and frustrated housewife of A Special Day could not be more different to Antonio and Robert, naturally, but in Macaroni there is an equally beautiful meeting of souls. The chemistry shines through and both work sweetly against each other.

It helped that Lemmon and Mastroianni knew each other before hand, though they had not spent much time together and were only vague friends. Lemmon recalled later that Marcello wanted to grow a real moustache for the film, and when Scola insisted they use a fake one, Marcello was adamant that he wear the real thing. Production shut down for a week, in which time Marcello grew his facial hair. When it came to the first day of the shoot however, he was embarrassed to

admit he had accidentally shaved it off that morning in an act of habit. Scola laughed and a fake moustache was ordered in. Lemmon admitted that such a cock up would have caused uproar on a Hollywood set, and he was pleased with the more laid back attitude of the Italians.

Macaroni is a joyous experience, a film it is impossible not to smile at. It has many standout moments, but there really are too many to mention. In all it's a brilliantly played mini farce with two outstanding performances leading it. Scola, once again, directs with grace, and some of his sequences, orchestrated in his usual precise style, are utterly breathtaking. The end sequence alone should ensure Scola is remembered as one of Italy's finest filmmakers.

In 1988 Marcello Mastroianni was back with Ettore Scola once again for Splendor, which cast him as Jordan, the manager of a cinema about to go down the pan. Marcello looks back on his life, first coming to the town of Splendor and opening the theatre which is now sadly ailing. Marina Vlady plays a showgirl who he frees from her tyrannical boss to work for him as an usher and whom he falls in love with. Their love story is told,

like the glory days of the cinema and his childhood memories, in the kind of crisp black and white one associates with the Italian Neorealist movement, and Scola achieves this effect wonderfully. The story changes with film geek Luigi (Massimo Troisi) who arrives to firstly swoon over the showgirl and then work for Jordan as a projectionist.

The film is clearly a critical look at the way TV has overtaken cinema in the heart of the public, a little like Fellini's Ginger and Fred, only much subtler and more restrained in its approach. While Scola laments the loss of film's power by showing Fellini's Amarcord among others, then the decline in ticket sales, he contrasts this with a rise in reliance on TV. There are even references to Mastroianni's past, with the likes of La Dolce Vita and Fellini. But the film is not weighed down by this message, and tells a good story which keeps you hooked. It is, however, a warm tribute to the world of film. As Mastroianni says in the movie, "Cinema is like a kind of great beyond." As for Mastroianni, he carries his past with him in a splendid effort, one of his most effective latter day creations. His past is with him at all times, and he can feel the traditions

slipping away from him, both his love and his work. Marcello holds this, once again, behind his eyes, which are filled with a quiet sadness.

Scola's direction is masterful here, and some of his choices are particularly inspired. The way he mixes up time and eras, often in colour then in black and white, is cleverly applied, reflecting the irregularity and randomness of our own recollections, which are usually presented too tidily in regular films. Here, Scola reflects the inconsistency of memory, the relativity of time, with its nostalgia and rose tinted glasses. It makes for a bittersweet, though not remotely schmaltzy mood throughout the movie.

Massimo Troisi is equally important as Marcello. The wide eyed, naive hopeful, desperately in love with cinema, stands for idealism, the fact that cinema is great with a capital G and that it can be powerful again if only people would switch off the mind numbing TV, get out and buy a ticket to see a movie. One scene in particular sums up Troisi's role in the film. Disappointed that only a handful of people have showed up for a Saturday afternoon screening, he goes over the road to a bar where a group of men sit at tables, not speaking or conversing, but staring into empty space. Troisi confronts them about their smugness, their complacency that they are all right without cinema, and don't need such a thing to fill their supposedly fulfilled lives. He mocks them openly, but as their passion cannot equal his he gets no real reaction. Cinema is dead, or if not dead, then dying. One man even pulls out a TV guide and tells Troisi it's pointless going to the cinema because there are so many movies on TV, listing Welles and Chaplin films scheduled for airing that very day. When Troisi asks which one he will be watching, the man replies none.

Again, though Splendor has a message about a culture void of worth, a generation reliant on TV, it works as a poetic story in itself, and hopefully even a big fan of TV and all its mush could enjoy Splendor, if not for its message, then at least for the story and the relationships between the characters.

Marcello, Scola and Troisi enjoyed their experience on Splendor so much that the very same year they hooked up again for an old idea Scola had been toying with for some time, the low key and very effective What Time Is It?

(1989). In some ways an ever more enjoyable film than its predecessor, it is well worth seeking out for admirers of all three of its key figures.

Massimo Troisi stars as Michele, a young man stationed in a small town army barracks, who meets up with his father, successful lawyer Marcello (Mastroianni), and with whom he begins to roam the town. They walk the streets, sit by the harbour and go shoe shopping together. The day begins pleasantly enough, though there is an underlying tension. As the day goes on, certain emotional difficulties reveal themselves, very subtly I might add, and Troisi reveals a preference for communication with the mother over his money minded though admittedly kind father. Marcello gifts him an apartment in Rome, where he can explore his apparent literary ambitions (in reality he has none), but the son seems irritated by the gesture. He also informs Michele he has bought him a car, which further puts him ill at ease. The one gift he covets most is his grandfather's pocket watch, which confuses Marcello no end. Michele does not want riches and extravagant presents; he wants love and realness.

Marcello meets his son's girlfriend, a kooky character he is not overly won over by, and also visits the coastal cafe bar where Michele spends much of his time and hopes to work once his military service is over. Marcello, wishing his son had loftier ambitions, feels like he is spending the day with a stranger, saddened by the fact the old man who runs the bar knows more intimacies about Michele than he does. As the past is dug up and certain antipathies come to the surface, the father and son confront one another but eventually reach a kind of truce, and though it is not a tied up, corny Hollywood ending, we are treated to a satisfying and fitting finale.

Everything about What Time Is It? works extremely well. Scola's direction is unfussy, intimate, and it is in the little details where he excels. He floats between the two men as if a stranger following them in the streets or eavesdropping during their meal. One of my favourite scenes is when Marcello is telling his son about the war, and Michele observes close details of his father's face; his wrinkles, the bags under his eyes, his grey hairs, almost as if he is clinging on to him while he is

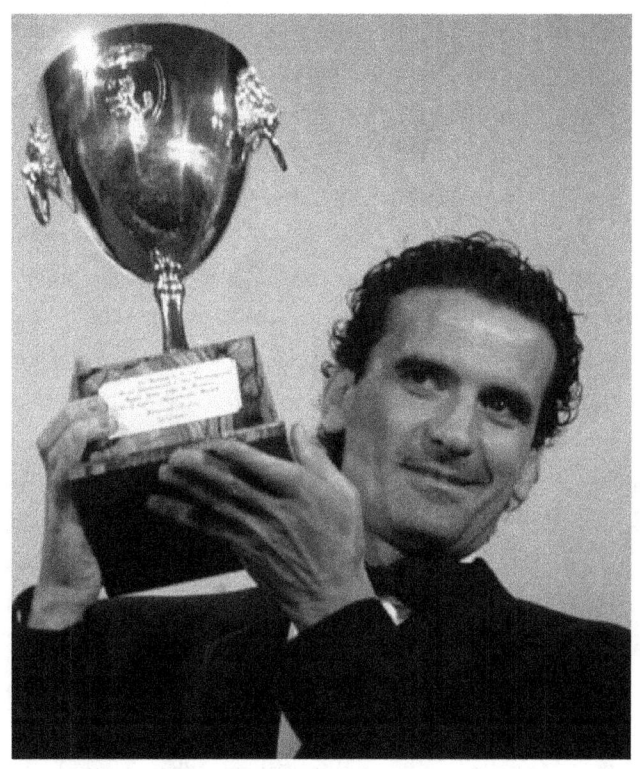

thinks of camera angles and shots few others could, and it is these choices which make the film more evocative.

The script too, by Ettore, Silvia Scola and Beatrice Ravaglioli, is consistently effective, never over cooked, always controlled and clearly conducive to stellar performances. Troisi is appealing as the modest son who just wants to be happy but has to live with his father's high expectations. Marcello, too, is paradoxically brilliant. Never an actor to rely or lean back on clichés, he is at once warm and distant, a man who wants a good relationship with his son but is aware that he has taken too long to get to know him. It's a balance he pulls off with expertise.

What Time Is It? is another vastly undervalued flick for Scola. It may be relatively well liked in Italy, but overseas is it very obscure. This is indeed

here, relishing his company and the most minute intricacies. It's a very poignant moment, but the film is chock full of them. Another highlight comes when they visit a small fair by the sea, and the pair of them each go on chintzy rides made for infants, engaging in passionate conversation face to face from their respective seats. In another lovely detail, for a few seconds they are observed from the revolving perspective of a grandfather who is standing on a merry go round with a small boy. Scola

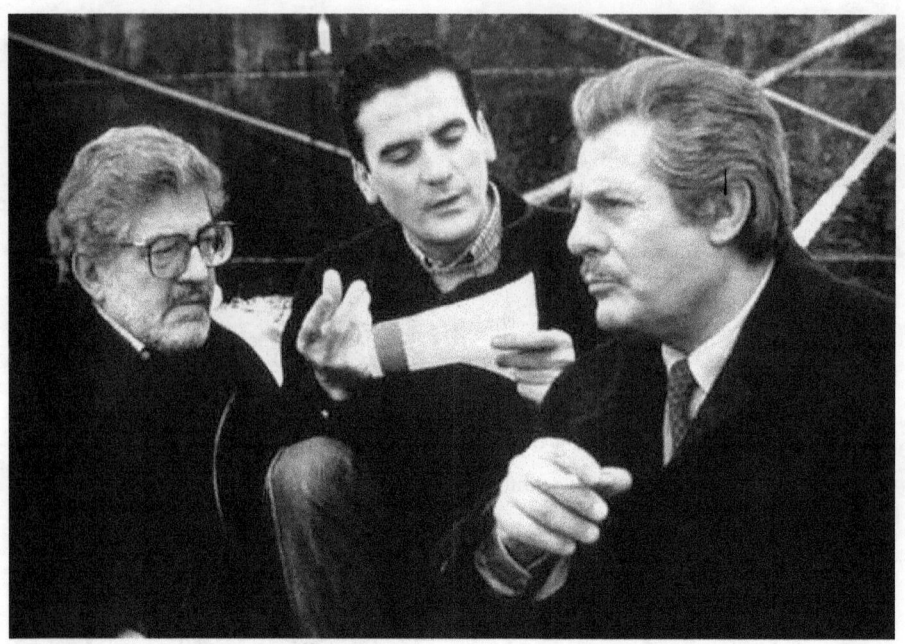

a shame, for What Time Is It? is one of the most quietly compelling and watchable films of the 1980s. Like Splendor, it pulls you in from the word go. Stripped back, mostly focusing on the two men (though there are minor cast members who are memorable, such as Anne Parallaud as Troisi's girlfriend) it is a lesson in grace. Never stooping to melodrama or schmaltz, it is one of Scola's finest hours. The soundtrack by Armando Trovajoli is wonderful too.

At the time of release it was met warmly and received various awards. Troisi and Mastroianni both earned Best Actor gongs at the Venice Film Festival and were nominated at the Silver Ribbon and David di Donatello awards. Scola himself won the OCIC Award at Venice and was nominated for a Silver Ribbon, though he deserved much more in my view.

Scola's last true classic was 1993's Mario, Maria and Mario. Valeria Cavalli recalled to me her memories of working with Scola on the film: "Working in Mario, Maria and Mario was a special and very pleasant experience. When I watched the film for the first time (and still now after all this time), I was surprised by certain things I had done without realizing I was doing them. To

75

maintain our spontaneity, Ettore didn't ask us to prepare the scenes in advance.

"As can be understood from his films, Ettore Scola was a great scholar of human behaviour, therefore also of his actors and he knew how to bring them, without their knowledge, to the right psychological conditions of their characters. He used many gimmicks to get there; Ettore was an excellent manipulative director (in the best sense of the term): in my opinion, one of the most beautiful encounters an actor can make.

"For example, the day we shot the scene of Maria disputing with Mario seeing a political rally on television. At the lunch break, Ettore imperceptibly introduced a topic for which he knew that Giulio Scarpati and I disagreed; by temporarily interrupting our complicity as actors, he made us exactly like Mario and Maria at that moment in their life: two people who "find their sight" and suddenly feel like two strangers, so we played the scene with a mixed background of grudge and regret. For this reason, I always say that the prizes won by the actresses are prizes that Ettore Scola should have won for his fantastic work on them."

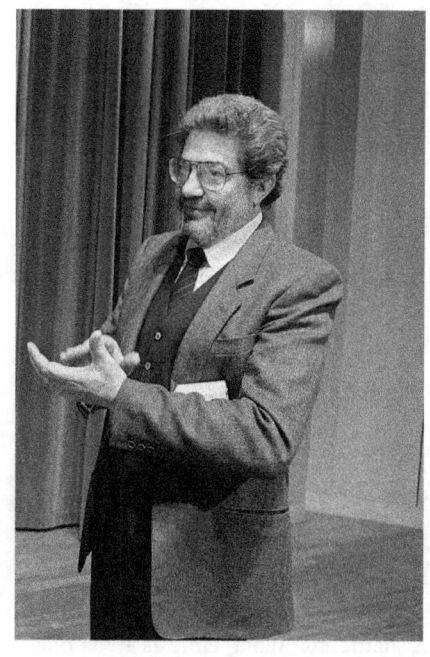

He was a director that got himself and the viewer totally wrapped up in whatever situation he was exploring. Ettore's films were often very moving without being corny or emotionally manipulative, and they were also relatable, realistic and so subtle it was as if we were watching real life. His directorial style, too, made it feel as if we were among the characters, not just viewing them on a screen. In What Time Is It? for instance, we are almost invading on private moments between the father and the son; in Ugly, Dirty and Bad (1976) we feel equally uninvited,

76

and somehow guilty for observing such vile squalor; in That Night in Varennes, we are among the sophisticated folk of the late 1700s, especially in the carriage scenes where Scola's cameras moves like an eye from face to face in the intimate surroundings. His films are never from a distant or satirical viewpoint, but through the feeling, sensitive gaze of a human being observing other human beings.

When Ettore retired, he admitted he was not concerned with having his voice heard any more, was insistent that he was not arrogant enough to assume the world was waiting for his latest film, and that he was happy to step aside and let the younger Italian filmmakers, who he believed had already started to make questioning, objectionable films about society, step in and take the batten.

"I was about to shoot a film with (Gerard) Depardieu. Everything was ready but in the end I didn't feel like doing it anymore," Scola said. "I didn't want to become one of those old ladies who wear high heels and lipstick just to keep youthful company. My experience in the film-making world is not what it used to be: easy and happy. There are production and distribution requirements that I can no longer identify with."

Rather than sticking around and falling victim to the modern film climate, struggling with the shift in the industry as Fellini did in the end (Federico found it increasingly difficult to finance his work as the 80s and 90s arrived), Scola withdrew gracefully. Through the dark downturn period in Italian cinema through the 80s, it is remarkable that Scola was even able to keep working at all; the fact he did so for so long is a credit to him.

When at his best, Ettore Scola often reached heights even his greatest and most famous contemporaries could not hope for, yet he remains unjustly underrated outside of Italy. Like Fellini he was concerned with people; unlike Fellini he inhabited a literal world of drama and conflict, whereas Federico stayed in the surreal landscape of the subconscious. Scola, it seemed, could turn his hand to any style, any genre, any backdrop. When he died in 2016 at the age of 84, cinema lost one of its most talented directors.

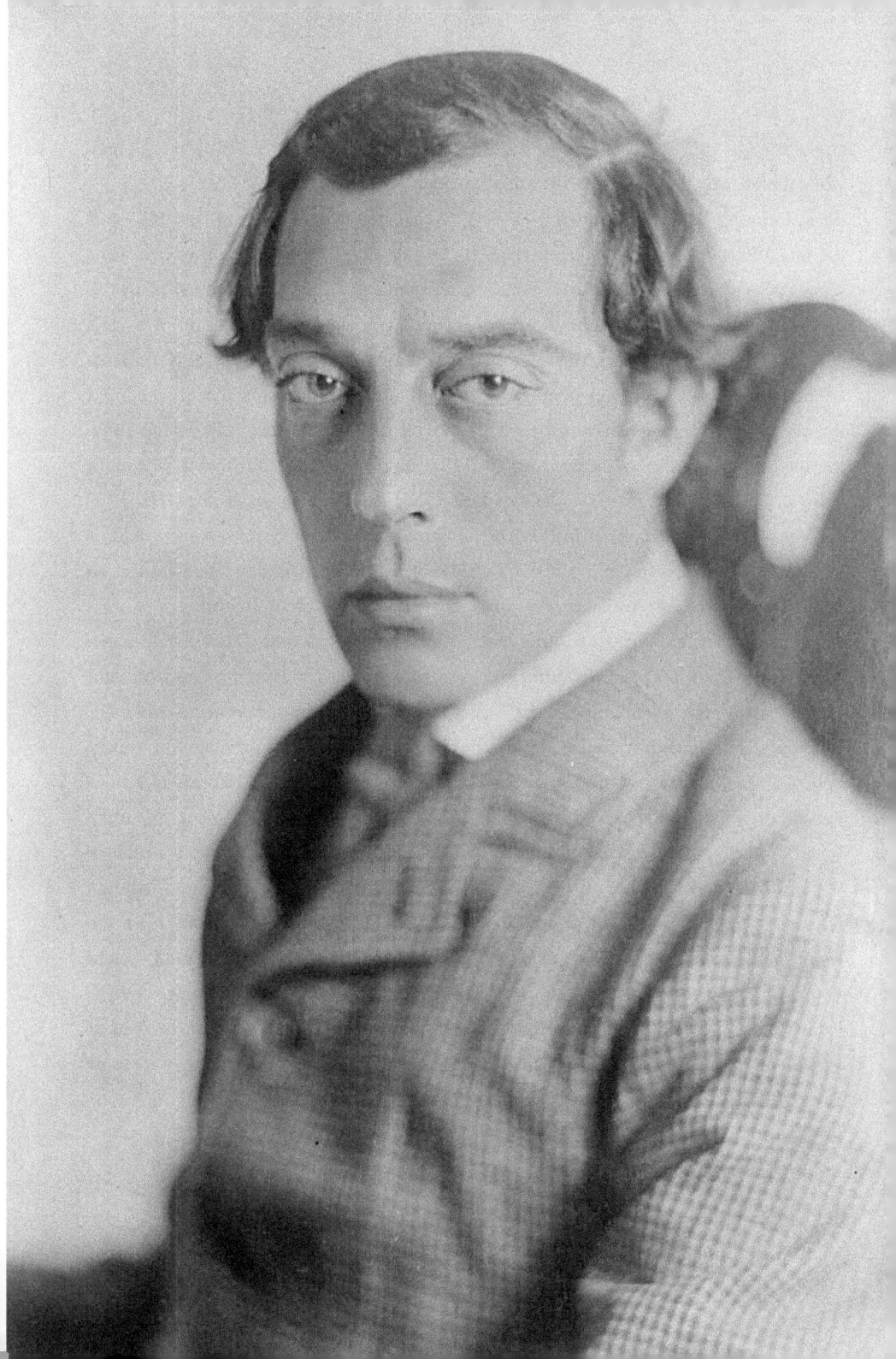

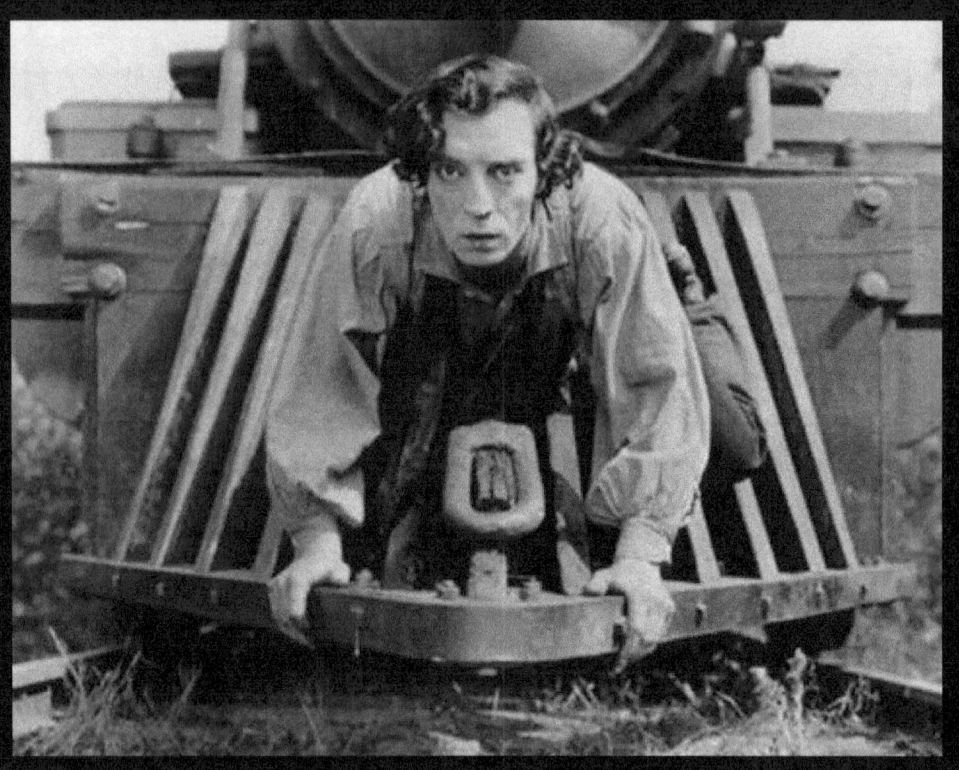

SALUTING...
BUSTER KEATON'S
THE GENERAL

Undoubtedly one of the greatest films in
American history, and largely recognised
as such, Keaton's masterpiece has lost
none of its awe inspiring power...

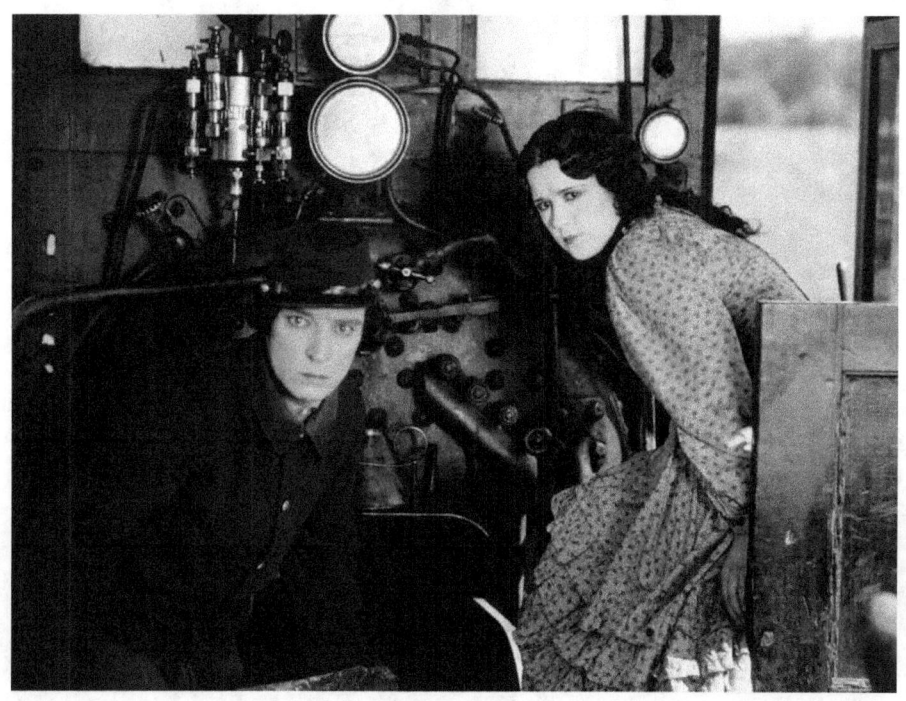

Though those only casually knowledgeable of the cinema of Buster Keaton may think The General is perhaps the only masterwork in the filmmaker's canon (indeed, it is often highlighted as such), they would be very much mistaken. Before he embarked on this spectacular feat, released in 1927 to little fan fare in its day though now regarded a classic, he had enjoyed a run of similarly impressive works. Though beginning his screen career as a sidekick to Roscoe Arbuckle, he'd rocketed into the twenties as a star in his own right with a series of remarkable shorts. Like Chaplin, he made his best work under his own production line and in his own studio. Buster Keaton Productions saw a ream of classics from Three Ages and Our Hospitality, to Sherlock Jr. and The Navigator. In this era Keaton perfected his awe inspiring physical prowess and became the only director of the time in comedy to get anywhere near Chaplin. Even today it seems impossible that Keaton could achieve what he did, but it's all there in black and white, special effects free. Whatever you see Keaton

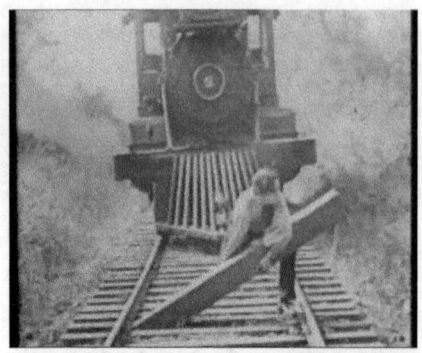

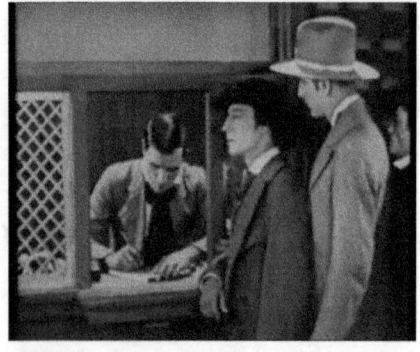

climbing on, jumping on or falling off, he did it all for real.

Anyone worried that Keaton's run of perfection might have run out of steam at the time could not have been more wrong. As Chaplin began to take longer over his passion projects, Keaton soldiered on full steam ahead. Just as it seemed he could get no better, along came the monumental The General. Inspired by the Great Locomotive Chase during the American Civil War, it was also lifted form the book by William Pittenger about his adventures on the railroad. It was Keaton's friend and collaborator Clyde Bruckman who first brought the book to Keaton, and always a train history buff, he was inspired to make a new picture. After changing around some historical facts, Keaton tried to hire the actual General train for the movie, but the owner refused. Still, he didn't let this stop him.

Filmed in Oregan, where some old time railroads still existed, Keaton had found the ideal destination for his true masterpiece. Arriving in May of 26 with their mass amount of props, filming was proposed to start shortly after departure. This was self-indulgence of the highest order, with Keaton at the steering wheel of one of the most lavish and expensive films of the era (filming cost $400 an hour apparently); clearly, he was in his element. Keaton's extravagance was encouraged by the fact that producer Joseph Schenck was so into the film that he gave him nearly half a million to fulfil his grand, ambitious vision.

The assembled cast and crew began their filming in June of 26, though apparently Keaton dismissed and completely ignored his leading lady, Marion Mack, for the whole of the shoot.

He was too busy with his crew, literally having the time of his life, to be distracted by anything or anyone outside his zone of interest. Ever the mythical figure, it's been said that Keaton assembled mass baseball games between the crew and Oregon locals, all of whom agreed Keaton was good enough to be a pro. Still, reports to the studio claimed Keaton was crazy with power, building new elaborate bridges solely for the purpose of destruction as the budget flew into the stratosphere. Some reports even said it ballooned to over a million dollars; whether true or not, it's a fact there were repeated accidents and major fires frequently throughout filming.

Yes Keaton was committing comic gold to the screen, but even though The General is genuinely funny, it is in its stunts and set piece where the film stuns the most. The destruction of the train, definitely the biggest scene in silent comedy history, remains frighteningly intense and, dare I say it, plain bonkers, and Keaton's dare devil stunts on the trains are unmatched to this day. No one in their right mind would attempt such feats today, and in Buster's era his daring bravery was near supernatural.

At the time though, these shenanigans went over the heads of most moviegoers, the people at the studio and most of all the press. Variety deemed it a flop and said it was far from funny, perhaps missing the fact that Keaton was not attempting to make a flat out, broad comedy. The New York Times, also misunderstanding the situation, complained, "The production itself is singularly well mounted, but the fun is not exactly plentiful. This is by no means so (sic) good as Mr. Keaton's previous efforts". For other reviewers it sat uncomfortably between drama and comedy, in their views neither truly funny nor thrilling. This is certainly down to taste, but one fact is that The General, like much of Keaton's best work, lacks an emotional centre and the gut wrenching sentiment which made Chaplin's work so special to some, and so schmaltzy to others. There's a methodical brilliance to Keaton's best films, making them almost scientific rather than emotional. Unlike Chaplin, Keaton never claimed to be an artist.

Negative reviews are a given with challenging art, but research reveals that there are hardly any positive contemporary notices for The General.

The wide rejection dinted Keaton's self confidence and sense of judgement; after all, though The Navigator was his favourite, he was also very keen on The General. "I was more proud of that picture than any I ever made. Because I took an actual happening out of the history books, and I told the story in detail too."

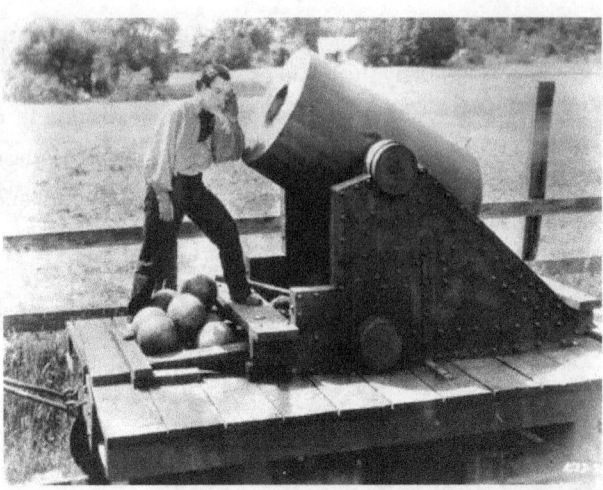

The General opened in two small Tokyo theatres while its US premiere was seriously delayed due to the successful Flesh and the Devil, a film taking up the Capitol Theatre for several weeks more than it was expected. Its release was delayed until February of 1927 and was dismally unsuccessful. For Keaton, it was a devastating blow, both to his ego and his reputation.

Today, not far off a century since it was put out to the public, The General sits in Keaton's filmography as Citizen Kane does in Orson Welles', a singular moment of genius that somehow, unexplainably so, turned out better than anyone could have imagined. All the elements were there, but the result was totally unexpected. Today, it's his classic.

The film's reputation started to change around the time Andrew Sarris wrote of Keaton and The General, in his book, American Cinema: Directors and Directions. "The difference between Keaton and Chaplin," he states, "is the difference between prose and poetry, between the aristocrat and the tramp, between adaptability and dislocation, between the function of things and the meaning of things, eccentricity and mysticism, between man as a machine and man as angel, between girl as convention and girl as ideal. There are those who would go further and claim

Keaton as pure cinema as opposed to Chaplin's essentially theatrical cinema."

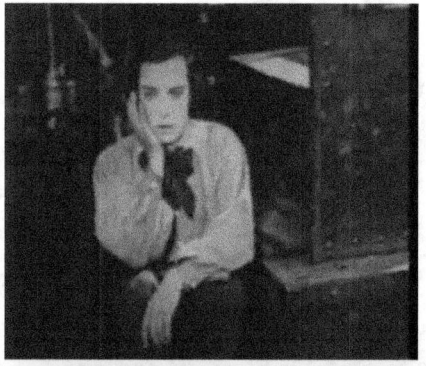

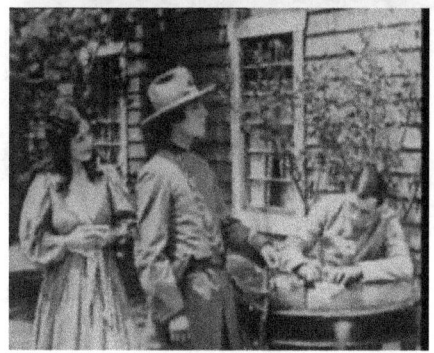

Years on from Sarris's praise, younger film buffs and writers have elevated it further. In 2014, Sense of Cinema wrote a piece on the film, and used it to define Keaton's current standing alongside his silent comedy contemporaries. "Of the three great American clowns of the silent era, Charlie Chaplin, Buster Keaton and Harold Lloyd, Keaton has emerged, by and large, as the cinephiles' favourite

over Chaplin, who was the greater star of his day and held the pre-eminent position in critics' eyes for the first half of the last century. Although both Chaplin and Keaton were remarkably gifted physical performers, Keaton's gags rely on a combination of his amazing physical abilities with the apparatus of the cinema – editing, pacing and camera placement. "

TCM recently summed it up nicely, writing, "When the Museum of Modern Art in New York scheduled a tribute to United Artists in 1955, The General was the only film so in demand it had to be shown twice. It was voted one of the ten best films ever made in Sight and Sound's international critics survey in 1972 and again in 1982. In 1989, it was one of the first films to be voted onto the National Film Registry, marking its official recognition as a national treasure."

The General, though not entirely representative of Keaton's pictures, is an awe inspiring achievement, and even in the age of modern CGI overload, there is a certain breathtaking quality to it. If only Keaton knew how his film was

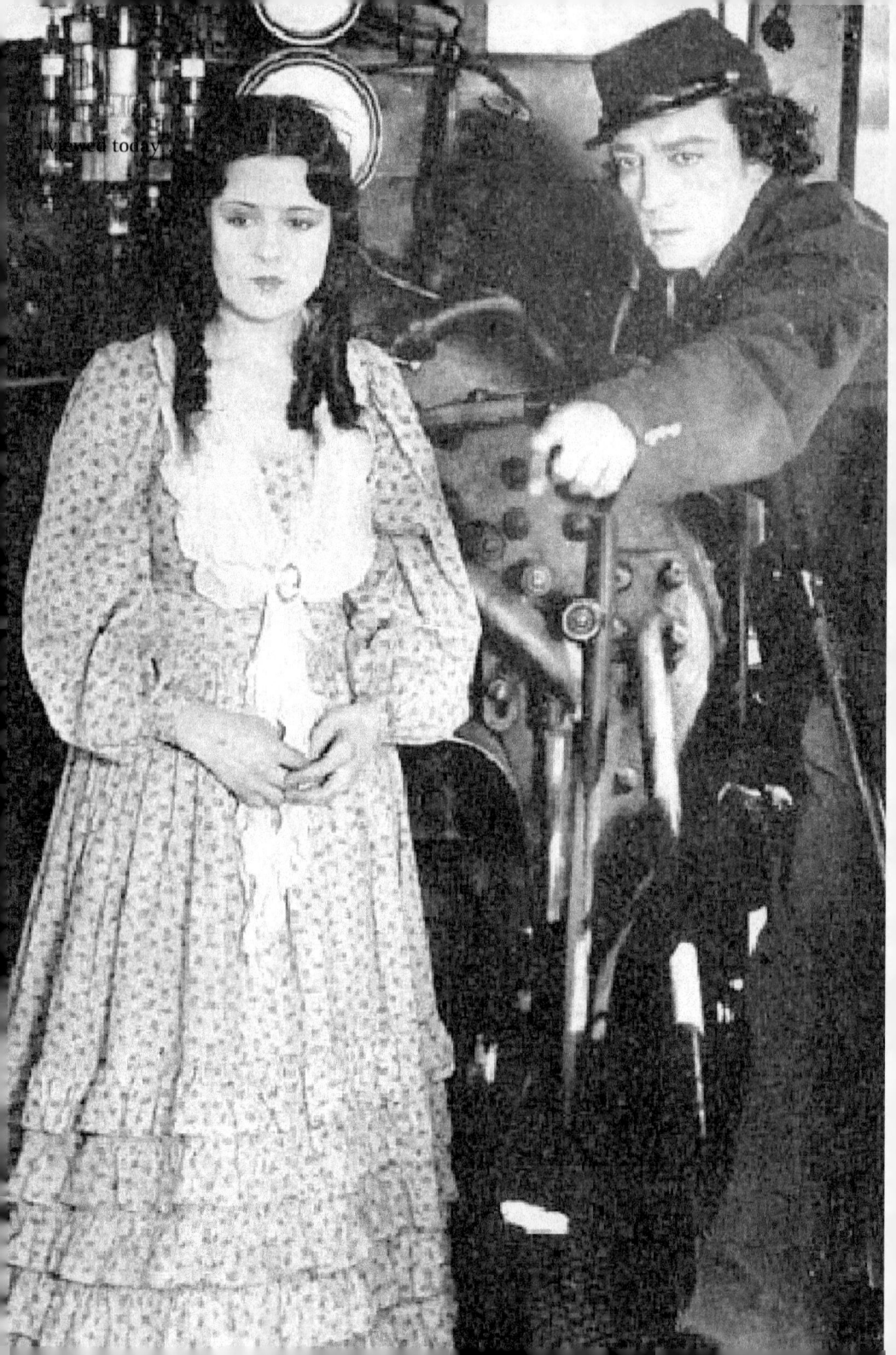

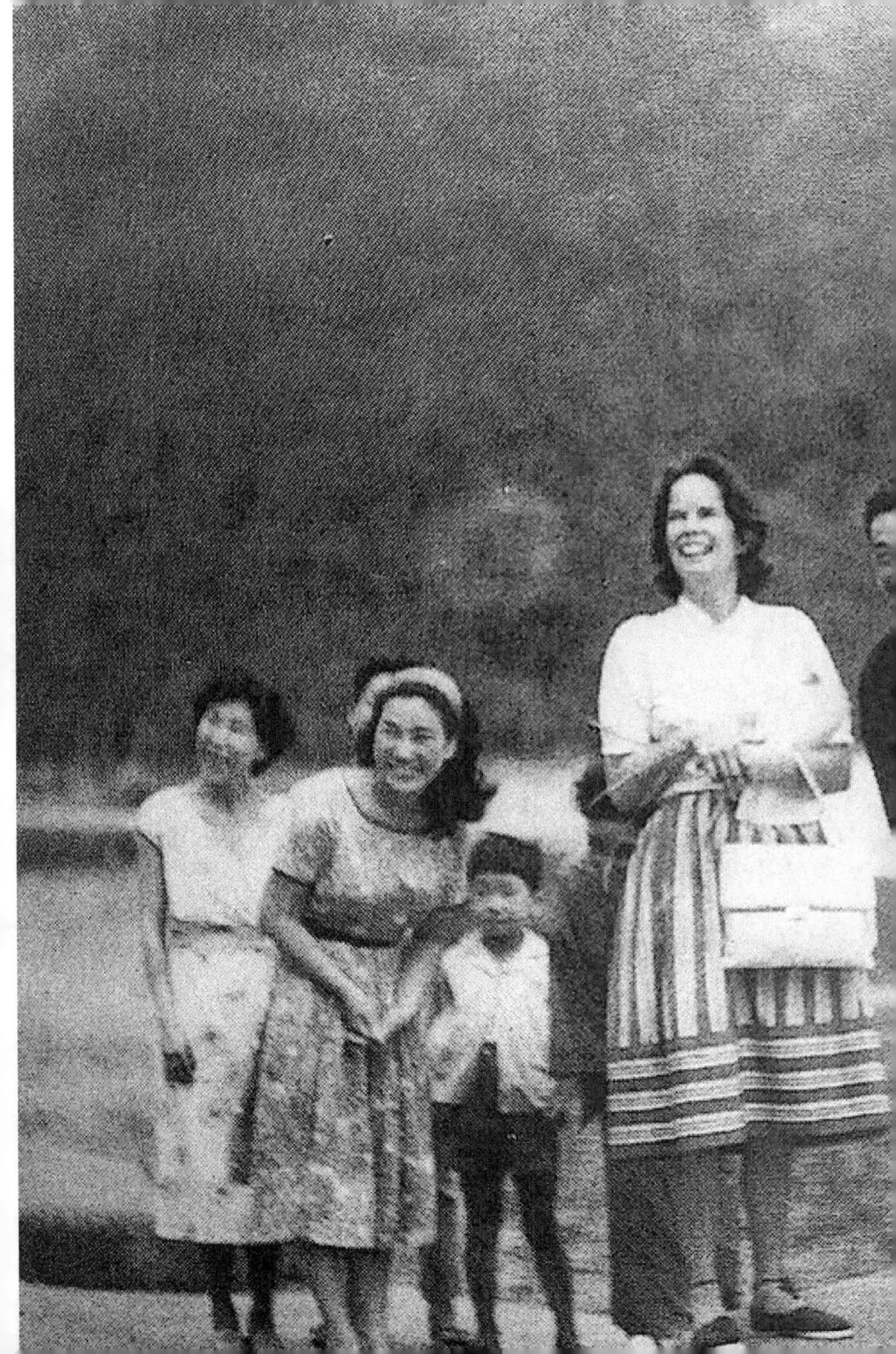

THE LATER YEARS OF CHARLIE CHAPLIN

CHARLIE CHAPLIN'S FINAL DECADES WERE SPENT IN SWITZERLAND AT THE MANOIR DE BAN IN VEVEY WITH HIS WIFE OONA AND THEIR CHILDREN. HERE, CHRIS WADE RECOUNTS HIS LIFE FROM 1960 TO HIS DEATH IN 1977

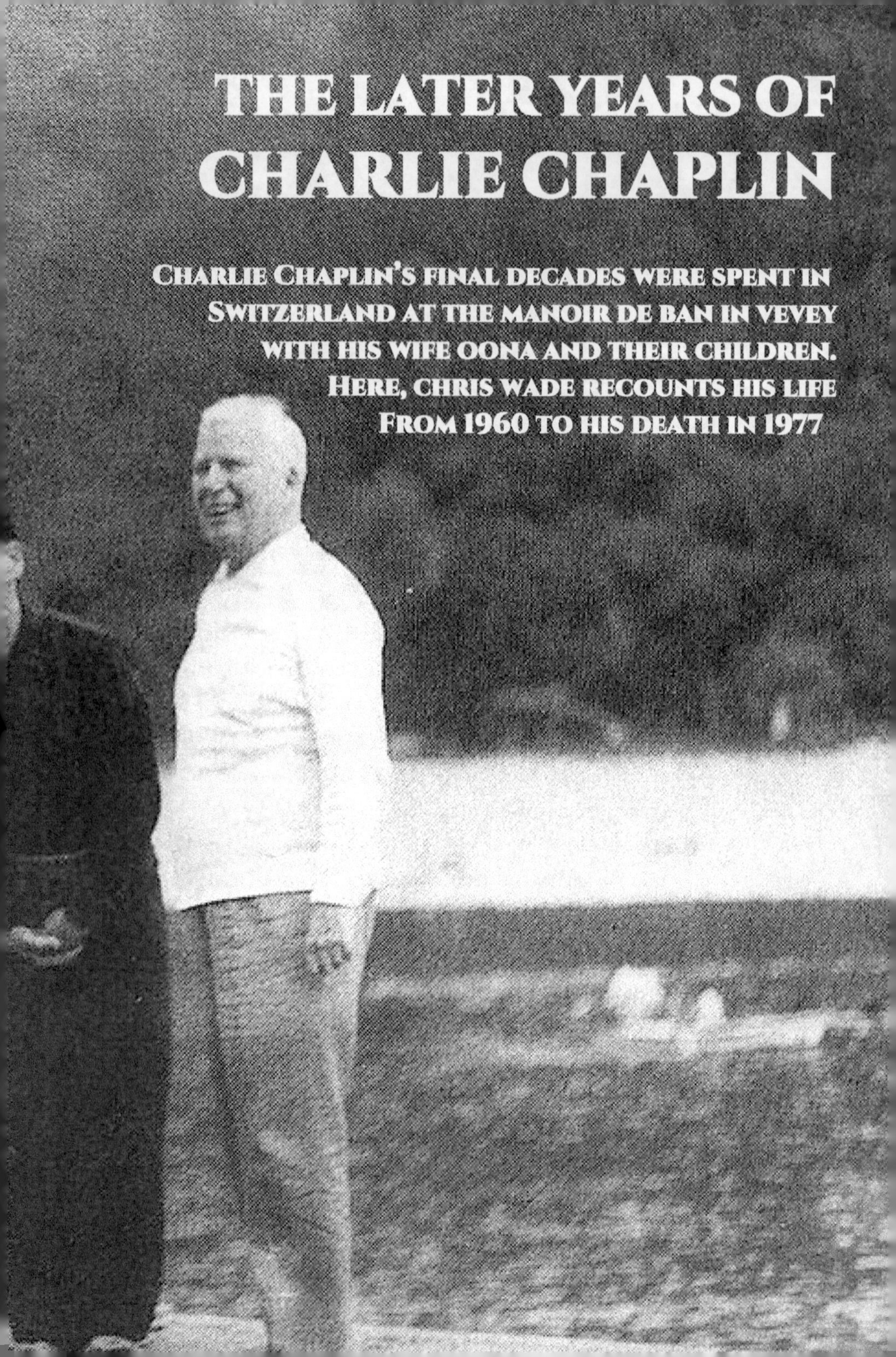

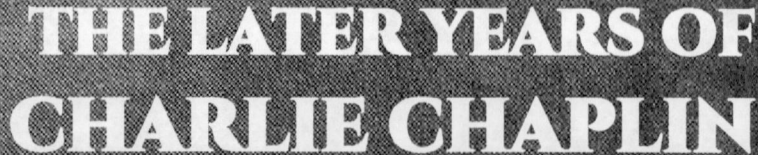

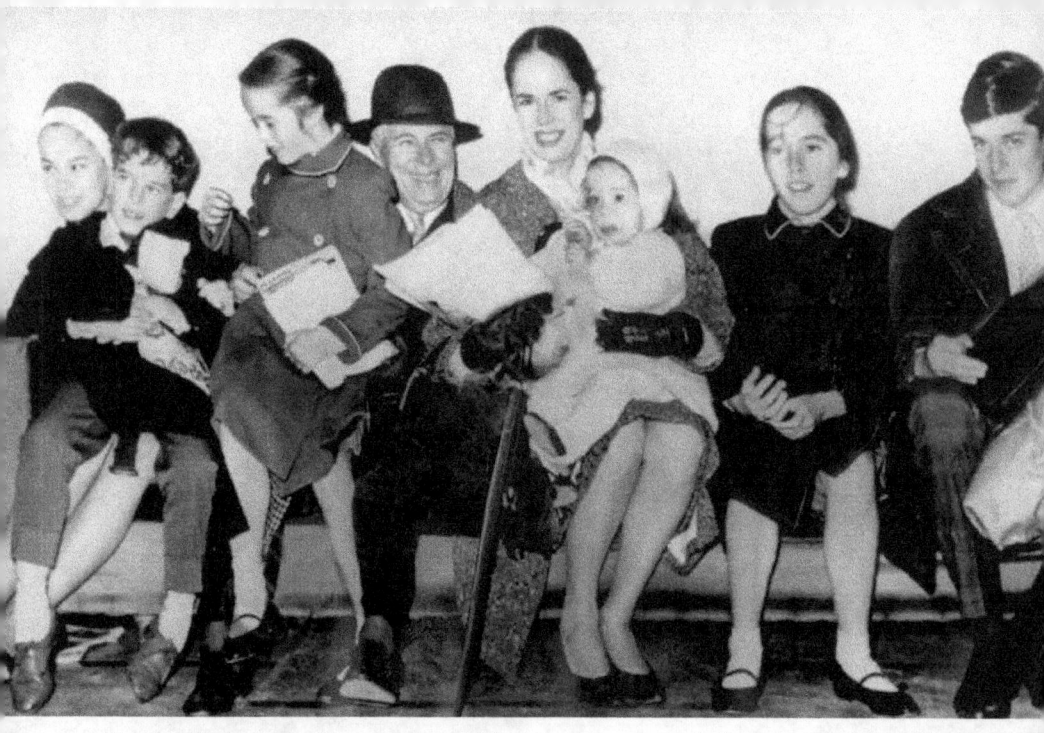

By the sixties Chaplin was surrounded by young children at the Manoir de Ban, and if home movies are anything to go by, he was having the time of his life. As his son Michael Chaplin later said, Charlie's earlier years had been all about work, work and more work. Now he was getting to play more often, even if films were still very much on his mind. Speaking in an interview, his daughter Geraldine Chaplin painted a portrait of what it was like to be a child of Charlie Chaplin: "Children have a very happy life in the Chaplin household. They play and laugh and sing and make a lot of noise all the time, and there's always something going on, an argument, a quarrel. And then mother gives them a lot of her attention, father loves them very much; children are never unhappy, never lonely in the Chaplin house. Everything's simple in the Chaplin household, while you're children."

"My mother was the backbone for my father. He depended on her a lot," younger sibling Eugene recalled, while Michael said she spent a lot more time with the kids and seemed more interested in what they were doing than their father. This said, Oona and Charlie were totally dependant on one another, and Geraldine said that the Manoir de Ban was their bubble, their little microcosm of their own. "Daddy was the

president and minister of interior, mother was foreign relation," Geraldine said.

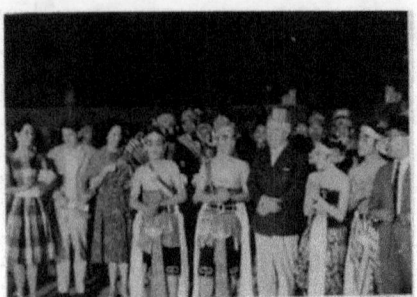

Chaplin attends a function in 1961.

Through 1962 Charlie and the family were all over the place. In the early part of the year they visited the Far East, while later the Chaplins went on a lavish holiday, taking in Venice, London and Paris. While in the UK Charlie was given an honorary doctorate by Oxford University. Speedily, Durham University followed suit and he was given a second degree. He was, of course, delighted. He took further joy in the arrival of his eighth child, Christopher James Chaplin, who was born in July of 62. At the time, Chaplin was 73.

Chaplin had many visitors at the Manoir de Ban that year, perhaps most memorably of all Frances Wyndham, who wrote about his visit and later penned an introduction to Charlie's 1974 book, My Life in Pictures. After a 1964 visit he wrote an article entitled "Chaplin At 73, Madly in Love." Wyhdham writes that whenever Oona comes shyly into the room Charlie grabs her hand and shows his adoration. He unashamedly interrupts conversations to declare his love for her. Wyndham also describes Chaplin as a "sensitive, proud, egotistic, touchy man, the essential artist." Frances writes that though Chaplin is an old man he still moves like a dancer. Revealingly, he also describes their private life. "Their front door is sometimes left open all night." Wyndham also says tourists approaching the house or milling about in the garden waiting for an autograph are greeted kindly and politely received. Clearly, he had not lost touch with the man beneath the mythical outer layer. One can only envy Wyndham when he writes that later on in the evening he sat with Charlie on the balcony, who then, as birds hopped on his chair arm, began to talk of his past. In the end though, the article dwells sweetly on Charlie's love for Oona. "It is because of her," writes Wyndham, "that he wants to go on living."

Many have said that Charlie was quite a strict father, though he was firmer with the older children than he was the younger, with whom he fooled and played around. Michael was the one who really rebelled, moving away at quite a young age to London, becoming a tear away, having a brief drug problem (from which he recovered) and writing a memoir based around his relationship with his father. Years later they made up of course, but having such a famous, iconic father was bound to be tough for a young man.

Charlie's half brother Sydney and his wife Gypsy continued to visit often, arriving in their caravan and staying over. His presence delighted the kids and brought out the performer in Charlie; home movies show the pair fooling around with the children. Geraldine recalled they would speak in pig Latin and cockney rhyming slang so no one could understand them.

Graham Greene was also a regular visitor. The pair had known each other for years, and enjoyed an on-off relationship. Greene's daughter later recalled her memories of sitting down with her father, Charlie, Oona and the rest of the children to watch The Great Dictator in the screening room.

Though he assumed the FBI and their prying eyes were away from him, Charlie later learned that even in Vevey he was being observed closely. The FBI, as had been proven in London in the previous decade, spread their influence across the globe and people were hired to photograph and keep tabs on him, some of whom managed to get close, take pictures when he was at his home or attending a public occasion.

Meanwhile, Geraldine Chaplin was just starting to make her name as an actress in her own right. But she admitted in one interview that inheriting the great surname was both a gift and a curse to an aspiring performer. "If you want to start a career, and your name is Chaplin, you don't have the slightest difficulty getting started. Everyone reveres you. Nonetheless the disadvantages are equally remarkable, believe me. If your name is Chaplin, people expect a lot of you. They expect too much and you must be good, you have to be, if you're not good they take umbrage, they make fun of you, their respect turns to scorn. But if you are good, they take it for granted and

whatever happens you never know whether it's to your own credit or due to your name. Oh! It's hateful to think that, if you do make something, it's just due to your name. It's hateful to think that, if you fail, you'll be crushed with shame: because of your name. There are times when I think it would be a lot easier to have an unknown name."

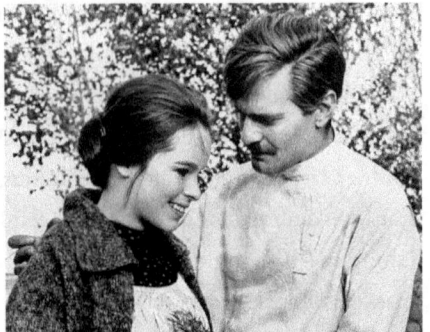

Geraldine Chaplin and Omar Sharif in Doctor Zhivago (1965).

Asked why she hadn't changed her name, Geraldine was firm in her reply: "Because I'm proud of it, obviously: very proud. Because I'm glad to be Charlie Chaplin's daughter. And also because it would be pointless to change it, it's too late. By now everyone knows who I am. Everyone recognizes me, apart from the fact that I take so much after my father and mother: I have mother's face from my forehead to my nose, and father's from my nose to my chin. Not only that: ever since I was a child I've been photographed with them all, and if I called myself Geraldine Smith, you know what people would say? They'd say: Geraldine Smith, Charlie Chaplin's daughter. The definition of 'Charlie Chaplin's daughter' will follow me all my life, even if I change my name a dozen times. And so, I might just as well go on keeping the name. The only trouble, apart from this positive obligation to succeed, is that you never know whether people give you a contract because they think you'll succeed or because you're Chaplin's daughter."

When the interviewer appeared impressed by all the screen work Geraldine had coming up, the young actress said "It's hard to say no when you are in demand and even harder when your father is Charlie Chaplin and he keeps saying 'do something, do something!' My father paid for my keep when I lived with a family in London, and now he pays or rather he was paying my rent of the flat I've been living in since I moved to Paris, But my father thinks that a girl of twenty should support herself, and I think so too.

Obviously I could always telephone home and say I'm in a mess, send me a cheque thank you, but I've never done it and I never intend to."

Geraldine also admitted that she was unsure how her father felt about her being an actress. "I think he's waiting for me at the finishing tape, to judge me... of course if I do fail, I shall face my father and tell him calmly I've failed father." She also hinted that once a child gets old enough they see the complications of having Chaplin as a father. "It's later that things become a bit less simple. It's later that you begin to think for yourself, see for yourself, decide to leave the nest. And so I've left the nest, Michael's left the nest... I was naturally, the first to leave it. After me it was Michael's turn and at present he's studying speech and drama in London. After Michael it will be Josie's turn, she's the beauty of the family, fantastically beautiful, even more beautiful than my mother."

While Charlie had looked back in 1959 when he put together The Chaplin Revue anthology film, he agreed to explore his life once more when he began writing his much anticipated memoirs. Records show he began writing them in 1960, taking the task seriously as if he might with a normal office job. He got up at 7 everyday, went for a swim, ate breakfast with Oona before kissing her goodbye to go to his study where he would write until midday. He would then have a nap, write again until 5 before having the evening off. Not content to write a lazy showbiz memoir, he wanted to dive head on into the furthest corners of his memory, especially those in London, bring to life the childhood struggles and contrast them with his often glamorous, star studded, but ultimately peaceful family life that came in the wake of his massive fame. Chaplin had considered a memoir as far back as 1950, perhaps triggered on by the Limelight novel he wrote and put in the archive, but by 1960, at that point with very little view of making another picture, Charlie was happy to sit and write. He was, as he said himself, "a content man looking back." He put his all into it, and always asked Oona what she thought about his latest passage. If she disliked one or asked him to get rid of it, he would go mad into a rage; but after calming down would always go with Oona's suggestions.

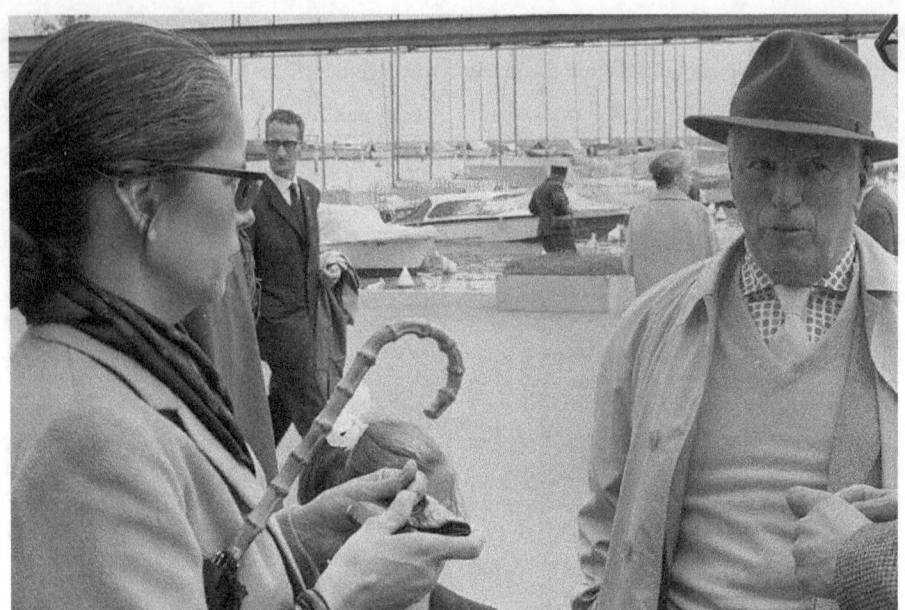

The book, simply titled My Autobiography, was eventually published in 1964 and was greeted by healthy sales and wonderful reviews. Dickens had been his favourite writer for some time (when he did learn to read, as David Robinson told me, Dickens' books became a major part of his library) and his influence on his own writing is evident. Indeed, throughout My Autobiography, though not concocting scenarios from his own obviously wild imagination, he gives real life events the kind of vivid detail and emotional power much of Dickens' work has. A man of images, famous for his films, had become a man of letters. Oliver Twist was a book that Chaplin read and re-read numerous times through his life, in particular near the end, and in many ways his memoir is his own Oliver Twist. Many have said Chaplin could have made a great screen adaptation of Dickens' rags to riches story of an orphan going through the grime and glamour of London life, one which sort of paralleled his own youth. In many ways, Chaplin lived Oliver Twist and it's all there in his book. Though at the time many questioned Chaplin's story and wondered how much of the childhood section was true,

subsequent research has shown his memory was spot on, and save for a few names mis-remembered, it's an accurate portrait of his early life. But it is a part of his life that remains so sad, so tragic, so unrelenting, that people may not have wanted to believe it was true.

Writing in New York Books upon the release of Chaplin's memoir, F.W. Dupee noted "His present life as described in My Autobiography resembles the last act of a late-Shakespearean romance. Order has been restored, love is requited, paternity is triumphant, and there has been a general reunion with the universe."

Indeed, there is true poetic beauty in the parts about his current life, Chaplin being a content man who has finally found happiness after years of misadventures. The best parts of the book for me are the early childhood memories and the present day section (Chaplin did once say he was effectively an "entrance and exit man", though he was talking about his screen work at the time). Sadly, the glory years are mainly covered in regards to his social life, all the great people he met and so forth, while little detail is left for his screen work and how he managed to create so

many masterpieces. But Chaplin said he was reluctant to give away details of his filmmaking techniques because it would undoubtedly take away some of the mystery and magic. He was right and though slightly disappointing in this area, the book nonetheless gets you inside Chaplin's head. While Peter Ackroyd in his short biography on Chaplin dismissed My Autobiography rather bluntly (funnily, Ackroyd's book itself felt as if written from a distance), David Robinson has praised it as the gem it truly is.

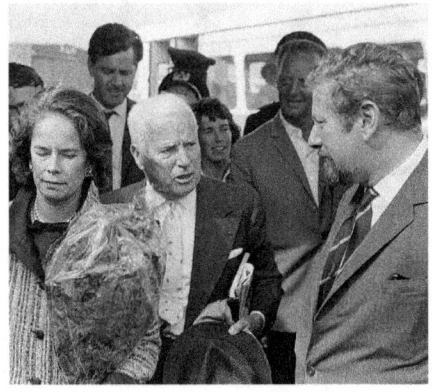

It was rather poignant that after writing about his youth and in part his relationship with his half brother, that Sydney himself should pass away. The man who had been Charlie's business confidant and very much his big brother, always out for his best interests, was now

gone. Ironically, he passed away on Charlie's birthday in 1965 at the age of 80. His wife, Gypsy, with whom he lived and travelled the world in a caravan despite his wealth, was later buried beside her beloved husband. The death shook Chaplin greatly.

That year he was honoured in Holland for his work in cinema. He told Peter Ustinov that he had won a prize but unfortunately had to share with a man he had never heard of. "I think his name is something like Burger... Ingman Burger." When Ustinov corrected him and said it was Igmar Bergman, Chaplin said "He's a Norwegian I am told." "No," said Ustinov, "he's Swedish!"

One would think that after all he achieved in his life, in movies and now in literature, that Chaplin - well into his seventies - should lean back and relax. Chaplin however was no ordinary man. It was after the release of his splendid book that Chaplin began cooking up ideas for his next feature, to be titled A Countess from Hong Kong.

You could fairly apply the word underrated to a number of Chaplin movies, given that personal favourites may not receive the same amount of acclaim as some of the widely lauded

masterpieces do, and opinions vary from movie to movie and person to person. But A Countess from Hong Kong is regarded by many to be one of Chaplin's weakest works, to some a slight misfire, and to others, and quite a lot it seems, an embarrassment all together.

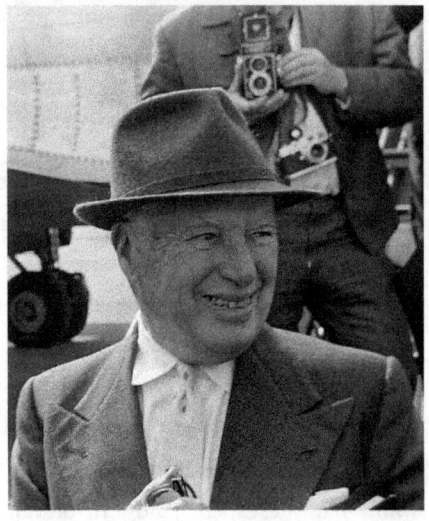

Chaplin greets the press in Holland, 1965.

Yet upon every viewing I have found the film entertaining, warm, and though far from perfect, both charming and funny, featuring a fine farcical scenario which moves speedily so and a host of performances which are competent considering the constraints put upon the actors in question. Yes the set up is old

fashioned, but it's brought into the contemporary sixties by two of the era's finest actors, Marlon Brando and Sophia Loren, who are broad but convincing for the most part. Chaplin directs with a refreshing simplicity and though the set ups often bring to mind the static staginess of television sitcom, while steering clear of cinematic fussiness, Charlie applies his masterly touch so well that 80 percent of it works.

Chaplin originally came up with the idea for the film in the 1930s under the title Stowaway, and it was based on a meeting with a Russian woman he met during a holiday in France in the early twenties. Chaplin also recalled he got inspiration from a 1931 trip to Shanghai where he met some Russian aristocrats who had escaped the revolution, "destitute and without a country." Chaplin said "the men ran rickshaws and the women worked in ten-cent dance halls. When the Second World War broke out many of the old aristocrats had died and the younger generation migrated to Hong Kong where their plight was even worse, for Hong Kong was overcrowded with refugees."

For his two leads, Chaplin chose two of the most loved and iconic stars of their day, Though he was not his first choice, he cast Marlon Brando as the male lead and after seeing her in the Oscar winning Yesterday, Today and Tomorrow, Italian beauty Sophia Loren as the female lead.

In the film which eventually surfaced, Brando plays Ogden Mears, the Ambassador for Saudi Arabia, who is on his way back to the United States on a boat when he meets the Russian countess Natascha, played by Loren, who has snuck on board after having enough of being degraded in a hall which promises sailors they can "dance with a real countess for a dollar". As Natascha is officially a refugee without a passport, she has to hide away in Ogden's lodgings for the rest of the journey. The situation becomes more farcical as the film reaches its end, and Ogden falls for the misplaced woman, who remains both earthy and dignified.

The word farce is key of course, because A Countess from Hong Kong is definitely a farce and nothing else. When one watches the film closely, you learn that little has changed from the chaos of Chaplin's earliest shorts, shot fifty years before this glossy production, only dialogue now helps drive along the

confusion and whirling mayhem of the film's mix ups and mishaps. There are some genuinely laugh out loud moments throughout, lots of energy which rarely falters, and Chaplin's brief cameo as the head waiter, during a rather choppy moment on the boat where everyone is being sick, is simply wonderful. It's his first and last moment on screen in colour, as well as his final movie moment all together.

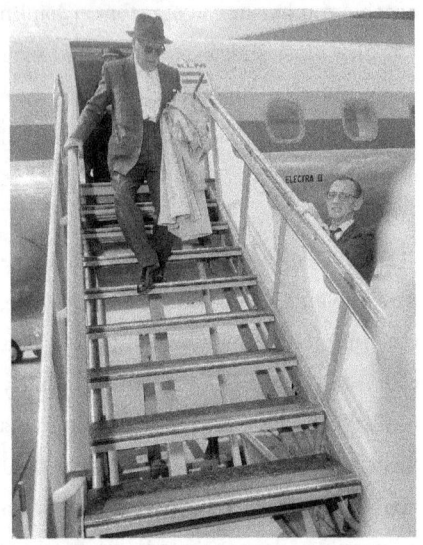

Brando, a man known prior to this for his visceral, tough and methodically constructed performances in films like On the Waterfront, The Men and a Streetcar Named Desire, applies himself surprisingly well to the more lightly comedic surroundings, though he does believably portray the more cantankerous side of Ogden better. He is clearly holding back, for Chaplin was famously dominant with his direction of the young method actor, yet he rarely falters in these controlled circumstances. Charlie's son Sydney does very well too, while the actor Patrick Cargill is a stand out in the cast as Ogden's valet, Mr Hudson, who delivers one of the film's funniest scenes when drunk and trying to get cosy in his bed. The real star, for me at least, is the beautiful Sophia Loren, a stunning spectacle in the middle of the slamming doors and scurried escapes, who is also very funny and effective with whatever Chaplin gives her in the film. Loren had started her decade with an Oscar win in the tough and enthralling Two Women, but here, as she did in some of filmmaker Vittorio De Sica's finest films of the 1960s, displays her knack with comedy. In truth she is the most comfortable and effective person in the film.

Unsurprisingly given her performance, Loren had a great time making the film. After all, Charlie Chaplin was one of her heroes, and she seems to have relished every second with the great man. In

2016 Loren said "I was so sensitive and scared to death. My God, Charlie Chaplin. What's happening to me? But I had to overcome so many emotions then went on stage and he was sitting by his wife. He was a very shy person and he was wonderful to work with and a great character. He helped every actor in every way he could. I still remember one day shooting a scene in a big restaurant and I was sitting down and there was a problem in the story, with Marlon Brando's character, and a very emotional scene with Marlon and after we'd done the scene Charlie Chaplin said, "For me helping to direct you, it's like I had my hands on the violin and just played the chords. You are wonderful." Listen to Charlie Chaplin saying this to me. I almost fainted."

Brando however, did not enjoy the experience. On his first day he arrived late, and an enraged Chaplin, pacing round the room impatiently, erupted when Brando finally rolled in. "If you're going to be late tomorrow, don't bother coming in again and I will get someone else." Chaplin had originally wanted Cary Grant, but eventually wound up with the less likely Brando, who, it must be added, decided to turn up on time everyday after Chaplin's telling off. "One day I arrived on the set about fifteen minutes late," Brando said. "I was in the wrong and shouldn't have been late, but it happened. In front of the whole cast Chaplin berated me, embarrassing me, telling me that I had no sense of professional ethics and that I was a disgrace to my profession."

He later called Charlie "a monster" and difficult to work with (in his autobiography he wrote that Chaplin was the most sinister man he had ever met), though Loren's account of the film's making in her wonderful autobiography could not be more different.

Tippi Hedren, who has a small role near the end of the film as Ogden's wife, recalled that Chaplin would act out everyone's parts before filming, clearly having the whole film mapped out in his head and being adamant that it would arrive on celluloid as close to that vision as possible. Brando hated this method, while Hedren admired it. "Chaplin's method was to act out all our different roles," she recalled, "which was brilliant to watch. Instead of directing, he'd get out there on set and say: OK, do this, and show us how. He'd become Sophia Loren.

He'd become me and Marlon. It was really unusual and I'd never seen it happen before. Can you imagine Marlon Brando handling that? Charlie and Marlon put up with each other, you might say. Marlon was so insulted to see someone acting out his role and that's why he wanted to leave. I thought it was charming and funny but Marlon wanted to quit and Charlie had to convince him to stay on. My take was, you have to look at life with a sense of humour, and the fact that Chaplin went out there and became our characters I thought was delightful. But Marlon wasn't thinking in those terms at all."

Future star of Monty Python, Carol Cleveland, had a small role in A Countess from Hong Kong as a nurse tending to Margaret Rutherford. In 2019 I spoke to Cleveland on the phone about her memories of the set and being directed by Chaplin.

How did you manage to get the part in A Countess from Hong Kong?

Well I got the call from my agent. I think we were filming at Pinewood Studios. I had been doing some work with studios then, and some TV and film bits, and it was my agent who put me up for the part. Whoever the casting agent was probably cast me in a number of things, so I think it was them who just cast me, basically, which was nice.

Did you meet Charlie Chaplin before you got on the set?

No, not before I went on set. And I was on set for a while before I did meet him, I remember. I watched from afar what was going on, a lot of technical stuff really when I arrived. Nothing was being filmed. I remember being very disappointed that Marlon Brando wasn't going to be there that day, because I was a tremendous Marlon Brando fan. But I was happy to see Sophia Loren was there. She was going to be in the next scene after ours. And I just watched her from afar. I did not meet her unfortunately. I hoped I was going to be introduced to her. But I watched her being made up and I just remember looking at her and thinking God you are stunningly beautiful. I thought she was gorgeous. So I did manage to see her but not Marlon. I did not see Charlie until we came to do our scene.

What was it like meeting him? Were you in awe or was it just professional for you?

Oh I was, I was in awe! Marlon, Sophia, all of them. After all it was early days in my career and I was always in awe of every film star I got to work with, because most of them were very pleasant. A couple weren't, but I won't go into it. But when he did arrive, he was lovely, Mr Chaplin. Margaret Rutherford had arrived at the same time for our scene together in the film, so they were setting all that up. There was a bit of time waiting around, as there always is. But then we came to the scene with Margaret, and that was very interesting. I did not have a lot to say in the scene, just a few lines as her nurse. But at the end of the day I was quite glad to have had only a few lines actually, because even though I go tot say my lines I was never too sure when and where I was going to be saying them. The scene was rather loosely scripted. I did discover much later on reading about the film, reading one of the reviews, and it said that was actually the way Charlie liked to work. With this particular film anyway, he had a very loose script and

he would stand there and go over it with the actors, and then there would be lots of improvising. And when you watch the film I think that becomes quite clear. In this particular scene with Margaret, bless her, there was a lot of fussing and faffing, and mumbling going on. The dear lady. And with Charlie, we ran through the scene a few times and each time it was different, totally different every time. Charlie was quite happy with what we were doing, me and Margaret, so then we went for a break. We had to do it a few times, and as I say it was never quite the same. I never knew quite when she was going to say her lines. I never knew when I was supposed to say mine. It was a very interesting experience. I remember giggling a lot to myself in between takes.

Watching Charlie direct, even though it was loosely structured, was he still in command, having people running around and responding to his orders? Did he seem like that kind of a director?

I think so yes. I mean I was only there for the day, I just saw him doing the scene I was in. Interestingly enough there weren't a lot of people involved. I

think there was just one other person involved, the three of us in the scene which was not very long. But as I say he was very calm and relaxed. He came over and basically said let's go through it a couple of times, and then said, fine, let's shoot it. And then it was just a case of faffing the way through the scene.

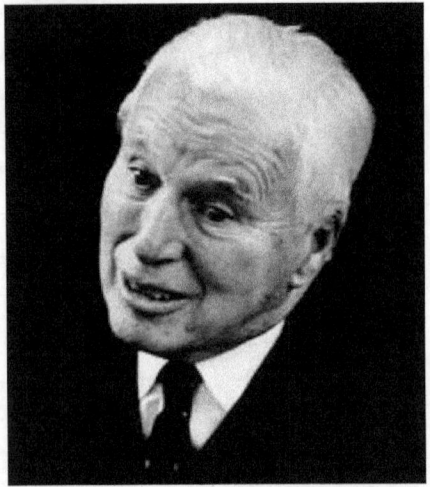

Was it surreal seeing him come into the room at all? Did it feel like this icon coming in from a different age?

I didn't think of it like that at all really. I was just, as I said, a fan who was delighted to be working with him, having already worked with his son (Sydney). I had had an introduction to the son, so now it was a case of I'm with the dad. And at the time I was more in awe of Marlon and Sophia, to tell you the truth. They were the ones I really wanted to see. But it wasn't until quite a while later that I appreciated how very fortunate I was to be directed by Charlie Chaplin.

Looking back on an experience like this - you are talking about being in a film with Chaplin, Brando and Loren for God's sake - does it ever feel like someone else? As if you ask yourself, was I really there?

I absolutely do look back and ask, did I really experience that? Prior to talking to you today I gave this some serious thought and thought, yes, even this morning, gosh I was lucky. I was so lucky to be doing that. I have been fortunate to work with a lot of big stars. Even though I was in awe, I wasn't star struck if you understand what I mean. Being in awe is different to being star struck standing there gawping. I just felt so lucky, and that's how I feel now, even more so actually.

The film was not a commercial hit and most of the critics despised it. To them, Chaplin was a man of the past and the

film was hopelessly old fashioned, stuck in another age all together. The New York Times were one of the most aggressive with their criticism, writing at the time, "...it is a far cry from the great films that Charlie Chaplin made, even as late as Monsieur Verdoux and Limelight, to the painfully antique bedroom farce he has put together in A Countess From Hong Kong. And if an old fan of Mr. Chaplin's movies could have his charitable way, he would draw the curtain fast on this embarrassment and pretend it never occurred. But that cannot be. We have to face it, not only because it has two such answerable performers as Sophia Loren and Marlon Brando in the leading roles, but also because Mr. Chaplin has indicated his great pride in it, and because it is being presented with splashy éclat. It is so bad that I wondered, at one point, whether Mr. Chaplin, who wrote and directed it, might not be trying to put us on—trying to travesty the kind of hiding-in-the-closet comedies, where people banged on doors and those in the room dived for cover, that were popular as two-reel silent films. But if he was, he failed to surround his story with a sufficiently clever slapstick style, and he certainly failed to communicate his intention to Mr. Brando and Miss Loren."

More recent reviews have criticised the acting, with TV Guide complaining, "Chaplin's story and script employed moth-eaten dialog and static scenes which none of the actors could enliven. Loren spends most of her time teasing Brando and the audience while wearing his silk pyjamas, running in and out of closets and toilets to hide, a peek-a-boo performance that is embarrassing. Her lines are delivered phlegmatically and are almost unintelligible through her thick Italian accent. She is earthy and peasant-like in a role that calls for sophistication and culture. Her unbelievability is matched by Brando, who struts about mouthing diplomatic ambiguities over what Loren's presence will do to his image and career. Chaplin's return to the movies is a sad failure..."

As time has it, A Countess from Hong Kong is viewed not as Charlie's last great heroic cry, but his final cowardly whimper. This is a shame, for I feel it deserves more credit than it unjustly receives.

Yet one cannot view A Countess from Hong Kong without understanding the

film landscape in which it was unleashed, especially if one is going to attempt to understand its harsh reception. Let us not forget, 1967 was the year of the arrival of New Hollywood, when Arthur Penn ordered the brutal and bloody on-screen massacre of Warren Beatty and Faye Dunaway's Bonnie and Clyde, when the mavericks snuck through the holes in the fence and temporarily took over the reigns of Hollywood's archaic chariot. In comparison to the new wave of films coming in to theatres that year, such as The Graduate, and the ones to follow, most obviously the likes of Easy Rider and Five Easy Pieces, A Countess from Hong Kong could not have been more stuffy and out of place. In the 1910s or twenties it would have come across as revolutionarily advanced in terms of plot development and camera sets ups, while it would have fit snugly in the Golden Period of the 1930s and 40s. In the mid to late sixties however, it's understandable, despite the vital talents of its two stars, that younger viewers found it unappealing. Thankfully, fifty odd years on, its appreciation has at least grown a little, though it will never enter the ranks of Chaplin's true classics. It is also worth noting that it is one of only two films Chaplin directed and did not star in, the other being 1923's A Woman of Paris, which was also funnily enough a commercial and critical disappointment. Had the films not been credited to Chaplin, then who knows, the critic's expectations might have been lower and the reception kinder.

That's not to say the film is flawless, for it is certainly flawed, despite being enjoyable. The final fifteen to twenty minutes for instance are a bit of a mess, while Loren and Brando's final scene together is unconvincing, especially with the overly sentimental soundtrack, written by Chaplin, intruding over the insincerity of Brando's delivery. Yet it's fun, daft and lovably corny. It's also Chaplin's final film, so whether perfect or not, a masterpiece or a dud, it's of major historical importance.

Charlie was understandably disappointed with the harsh reviews. He told Francis Wyndham during an interview that with his next film he wouldn't open it in London. "I will open in Kalamazoo or somewhere and leave London till later. " He went on to criticise London, saying he didn't understand what was going on there.

One must remember the London he was speaking of was in the midst of its so called swinging era. "When the swinging thing is over, what will they have left?" he asked. "I don't believe there is such a thing as fashion. Who the hell creates fashion anyway? Anyone can. Cynics - so what? Soon they will come to their senses and start having a good time."

David Robinson, noted film critic and future Chaplin biographer, had managed to get himself into various Chaplin press conferences through the fifties and sixties. He recalled being at the event Charlie hosted announcing his plans to make A Countess from Hong Kong, but admitted he didn't build up the courage to ask the great man a question. In the seventies however, after writing an article about the re-release of Limelight, and shedding some light (no pun intended) on the music hall backdrop against which the film was set, Robinson received a pleasant surprise. In 2019 he told me, "In the New Year I got a card in the post signed Charlie and Oona Chaplin. I thought it was a joke. People know I like Charlie Chaplin, so someone's having a gag with me. On the bottom it was signed 'We loved your review of Limelight, Charlie and Oona

Chaplin.' And then I thought, OK, maybe it's real! So I made so bold as to call the Chaplin secretary to say thank you very much and how touched I was. And then I forgot about that. Kept the card of course, still got the card!"

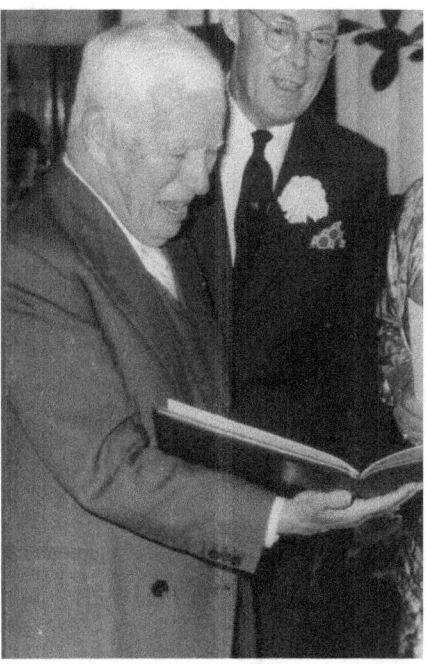

Charlie consoled himself by insisting the reviews for his films had always been mixed, and also noted the irony of the fact that the theme to A Countess from Hong Kong had become a hit all over the world. He mentioned admiring some recent films, such as Goldfinger, but thought the artier films, in this case Antonioni's Blow Up, was "slow and

boring", while also dubbing Doctor Zhivago, among the biggest films of the era no doubt, "banal".

Speaking to Richard Meryman in 1966, Charlie was willing to discuss his films but not his private life. He talked of his technical tastes, his set habits, but didn't give much away about the magic he had achieved. Bearing in mind he had just made a film in a completely different age and environment to what he was used to, Chaplin explained: "I like the lighting more or less up—I don't like shadows. I don't think it's the most important element in a film. I think if you concentrate on that, you may be neglecting something else. As to the camera, if I have a rule at all, it is the fact that I like to establish orientation— to know where you are. I like to keep the camera way back, then come into a close up or whatever you want to finish up. You can eliminate time, with discretion, but now they go overboard. I don't mind when they cut away—it's refreshing to me. But I do like to see something smooth. I use the close up, not in any sense of mechanics, but sort of as an emphasis, as punctuation, like putting in a comma or parentheses. Technique is so much a part of expression through the camera. But I really concentrate more on the performances of the actors."

On the fact that people might find him and his latest film old fashioned, Chaplin said "Well, they all have an idea that I'm terribly conservative and I'm not. We don't twist the camera upside down. Personality, people, the human equation transcend any acrobatics that the camera might do. I don't think there is such a word as being old-fashioned, in the deepest sense, because we don't understand the past, the present; we're conscious of the future. I like the misty mysticism of that. Time is something that is there, and we pretend that everything is modern and new, but it's not. So I'm never bothered about being old-fashioned. Of course, one is so insecure, because you never know what the hell is coming out. It was very fine, very discreet. I rather liked the idea of it. It's like any picture—the only nervous qualms I had was starting. The moment we took the first scene I knew what I wanted."

Meryman also brought up the word genius in his interview, but Chaplin was reluctant to apply it to himself. "I've never known quite what a genius was. I think it's somebody with a talent, who's

highly emotional about it, and is able to master a technique. Everybody is gifted in some way. The average man has to differentiate between doing a regular sort of unimaginative job, and the fellow who's a genius doesn't. He does something different, but does this very well. Many a jack-of- all-trades have been mistaken for a genius... but genius is such a pretentious word, and you come to find it doesn't mean anything. You see genius all over the world, in beautiful paintings ... I think they do their job well, and they're artists, and how far the genius goes, some are better artists than others."

Though Chaplin was not in his latest film, save for the cameo, interviewers still brought up his Tramp persona. Speaking of the Tramp's place in modern times, and perhaps addressing why he refused to play him any more, Chaplin said, "I don't think there's any place for that sort of person now. The world has become a little bit more ordered. I don't think it's happier now, by any means. I've noticed the kids with their short clothes and their long hair, and I think some of them want to be tramps. But there's not the same humility now. They don't know what

humility is, so it has become something of an antique. It belongs to another era. That's why I couldn't do anything like that now. And of course, sound—that's another reason. When talk came in I couldn't have my character at all. I wouldn't know what kind of voice he would have. So he had to go."

Though accommodating in interviews and playing down the harsh rejection of his film, friends and family say the reaction to the film, as acidic as it often was, hurt him greatly. The film also came out around the same time Michael published his warts and all memoir, which brought embarrassment to Oona and Charlie. Even though the book spoke of Chaplin's more difficult character traits, Michael insisted he adored his parents. He dubbed his father "complex, gifted, strangely creative... He was and is, to put it mildly, a bit of a handful as a father."

Things began to change around the time he was working on A Countess from Hong Kong. While editing the film, he went out for a walk with his friend Jerry Epstein in the grounds of Pinewood Studios and tripped and fell on a piece of crooked pavement. He was driven off to Slough Hospital where his

foot was put in plaster. Chaplin found the whole thing humiliating, and was perhaps aware that at his ripe old age (he was in his mid seventies) an injury like this could seriously slow him down. It was the first chink in his armour so to speak.

In 1967 the iconic mime artist Marcel Marceau had a chance meeting with Chaplin, the man who had been his childhood idol and helped inspire him and his act. While waiting for a plane at Orly airport, his cousin alerted him to the fact that Chaplin, Oona and the children were all sat in the airport cafe, and that Charlie was looking at him. When Marceau built up the courage to approach his idol, Chaplin said "Hello Marcel Marceau. I have seen all your posters in Paris. Children, come and meet Marcel Marceau." Marcel told Chaplin he was a God to him. He then began to mimic the Tramp walk, which prompted Chaplin to do the same. For Marcel it was a magical moment. When Oona urged Charlie to hurry up as they needed to be in Vevey, Marcel saw that Chaplin had tears in his eyes. Marcel saw it as a symbolic meeting. Chaplin had once been unable to move through the streets without being mobbed. "And then nobody recognised him," Marcel recalled. "He had not made films in years and I was not only Marcel Marceau the mime, but a new generation. When I kissed his hand, he thought about time, that he had no more life before him." Marcel saw the meeting as poetic, rather sad, and indeed Chaplin may have seen that his influence was going on into a new generation, that his legacy, as much as he might not have thought so at the time due to the onslaught he had received in America, was very much alive and well.

Towards the end of the decade a real tragedy struck him, the death of his son Charlie Jr. in 1968. He had been born in the mid twenties to Charlie and Lita Grey, and was only 43 when he died in his mother's house. The death, was with his brother Sydney, hit Chaplin hard.

Though Chaplin was a happy family man, he was still prone to melancholia; indeed, as he had at the height of his fame. Speaking of her father, Geraldine Chaplin recalled his mood might change in the festive period, where he was reminded of his sad childhood. "But on Christmas, while my mother was putting amazing presents under the tree

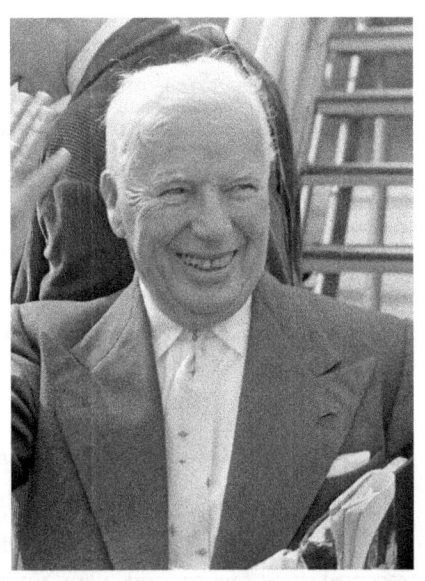

for me and my sisters, he sometimes grew melanchooly. He said, When I was a child, I got an orange. In good years. His most famous movie character, the Tramp, surely had something to do with that childhood. A completely destitute vagabond, who nonetheless has dignity and manners. For me, that character was always a transfigured version of my father's childhood story: the embodiment of a humanism that couldn't be broken. A man who always stood back up. And who always maintained a sense for beauty and romanticism."

That said, he continued exploring his next film idea, The Freak, which obsessed him for years. He started serious work on it in 1969, intending it as a vehicle for his daughter Victoria. The story concerned a young girl in South America who suddenly grows wings and is kidnapped. She finds herself in London where her kidnappers plan to make money out of their find. When the girl escapes, she is not treated with kindness, and because she is different, she is ostracised and treated like a freak.

Chaplin was deadly serious about The Freak and put all his energy into it, despite being 80 during early development. His family and friends knew deep down that Charlie just didn't have the energy to take on another film, but didn't have the heart to tell him. Even by 1974, when he published the wonderful My Life in Pictures book, the final image of him working in his study has a caption regarding The Freak, still insisting that he planned to make it one day. He had the wings made, took pictures of Victoria in costume and even held auditions in London for supporting roles. Charlie shot footage of Victoria in their garden wearing the wings, and Michael later recalled that his father got out of his wheelchair to tell her where

she was going wrong. "He became a film director again," Michael added.

But it was not to be. Victoria suddenly met a man, got married and moved away. Besides, she wasn't sure the acting life was for her. Alas, the film was never made; which is tragic, as documents show that it would have been another masterpiece, perhaps his finest film since The Great Dictator or even earlier.

"It seemed to me to be a very beautiful fairytale. Something that maybe only a man of his age can imagine, can dream. A very charming dream," Michael Chaplin told AFP in 2015. Author Pierre Smolik, who penned a book on the doomed project, said of the screenplay, "When reading it, one can glimpse what this 'Freak' would have been: a subtle mixture of the tale, the fable, the dream, the amusing, tender or satirical comedy, black humour, the tragedy, the nightmare, suspense, poetry."

Insistent he was still going to make it, even as frailty overtook him, the lost masterpiece tormented him and became buried in the sands of time. Still, the footage of Victoria in the wings, fluttering around the grounds of the Manoir de Ban, sends a chill up the spine and suggests what the film might have been had he taken it on ten or fifteen years earlier. The script was kept a secret for years and it became something of a myth to Chaplin fans.

Things were really slowing down as the sixties morphed into the seventies, and Chaplin, now aged 80, was beginning to slowly fade away. Though he was no longer seriously attempting to explore new film ideas, he was still very much invested in his old masterpieces. At the turn of the decade he was exploring new deals for the distribution rights to his films, with both Jerry Epstein and his son Sydney putting themselves forward as hopefuls to take over such affairs. One time Sydney turned up at the Manoir de Ban with the producer Sandy Lieberson, with a view of talking to Charlie, who knew nothing of the meeting, about possible sales abroad. Chaplin was offended by Sydney's forthrightness and the whole household erupted into an argument. Clearly, Sydney had crossed a line. Instead, Chaplin's secretary Rachel Ford set up a deal with Moses Rothman, who started a new company to distribute Chaplin's movies in the USA, where half of all proceeds would go to Chaplin's Roy Export Company. Once again, the

formidable Ford had stepped up to the plate. As part of the deal, Chaplin agreed to make the odd promotional appearance to support re-releases of his films, this also ensuring he had a continued interest in his past work and went on composing new scores for them. In 1971 he cut new scores for both The Kid and The Idle Class, and the music was as effective as anything he'd created before.

1971 was also the year the Cannes Film Festival decided to honour the great man. The French had always loved Chaplin, indeed had most of Europe, so such plaudits were expected. More unexpectedly was the 1972 Oscars tribute to Chaplin, organised by long time admirer Peter Bogdanovich. Chaplin did not see himself ever going back to America again, but now he was older a lot of the grudges had faded, and he was genuinely moved to be invited by the Academy.

Bogdanovich recalled the events which led to Charlie coming from Switzerland for the tribute evening: "Burt Schneider, who produced The Last Picture Show, was bringing Charlie Chaplin's pictures out again, for the first time in ages. So the Academy was going to help promote those rereleases by giving Chaplin a special Oscar. Burt called me and asked if I would do the montage of Chaplin clips to introduce Charlie's arrival back to this country after 20 years in exile. So I said Sure. I knew Chaplin's pictures pretty well, so it didn't take long. I went through the ones I wanted as an editor, and put it together pretty quickly."

As the montage was 13 minutes long, the Academy said it was too lengthy to be shown. Burt told them Chaplin would not come unless they screened the reel, so finally they agreed.

Bogdanovich recalled his other memories of Chaplin: "I had never met Chaplin before he came to Hollywood for the Oscars tribute, but we were in communication beforehand. In fact, he gave us all the old films I used for the clip reel. They came directly from Charlie. I actually sent him the montage to see if he liked it before I sent it to the Academy, and he came back and said he wanted a clip from The Great Dictator in it, because there wasn't one — it's not one of my favorite films — but he wanted a shot of the dictator bouncing the world as a balloon. So we put that in. And that was his only comment."

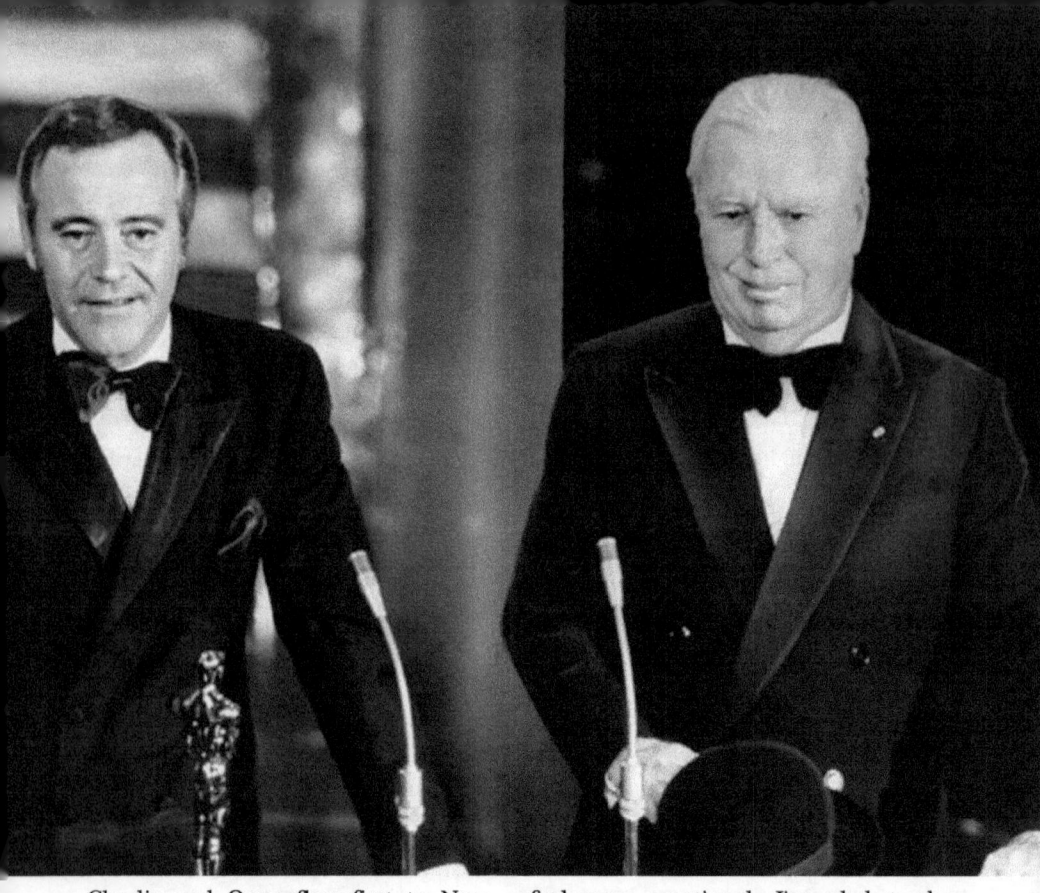

Charlie and Oona flew first to New York. Charlie had been nervous about coming to America but was overwhelmed by his reception. When they screened The Idle Class and The Kid at an event four days before the Oscars night, Chaplin was moved, stating from the stage: "First, thank you for your wonderful applause. It is so very gratifying to know that I have so many friends," he said. "It's easy for you but difficult for me to speak tonight, as I feel very emotional. I'm glad to be among so many friends. Thank you."

The next day he and Oona went through Central Park and had dinner at the 21 cafe. Old friends visited his hotel suite and the Mayor of New York gave him the Handell medallion, the highest honour of the city. He spent the rest of the week in the big apple before flying to Hollywood with Oona, accompanied by Candice Bergen who was writing a piece on Chaplin for Life Magazine. She reported Charlie's excitement when the

plane passed the Grand Canyon, and like a child he rushed to the other side of the plane to peer down at it. He began to feel more nervous as they got closer to LA. "Oh well," he was heard to say, "I did meet Oona there after all."

When he arrived he learned that the new owners of his old film studio had decorated the place with banners with Chaplin's face on them to celebrate his arrival. Apparently, overcome with emotion, Charlie could not face the greeting he would receive there, or the old studio itself where he had crafted so many glorious masterpieces. Later on, when it was closed, he went over and peered solemnly through the gates at his old work place.

At the weekend he lunched with old friends, some of whom he did not appear to recognise. Over awed by all the people around him, Charlie was having a few seconds chat here and a few seconds small talk there. Tim Durant, an old friend who was at the dinner, was upset when he assumed Charlie did not recognise him. However, near the end of the event Charlie leaned over and quietly said "Tim, you and I were friends once". Tim was terribly moved by the moment.

Then Charlie built himself up for Oscar night. Once again, Bogdanovich had vivid memories of the evening: "Then the Academy told me that Charlie couldn't walk down the stairs, so I just said why don't we have the screen that shows the montage fly up at the end and he's just standing there? The place will go nuts. So that's what they did. Thirteen and half minutes of film ending with a four-minute sequence from The Kid which would make a stone cry. Believe me, I was there, the whole place was crying! It was this heartbreaking scene between Charlie and young Jackie Coogan. And then the final shot was the last image of The Circus, when Charlie just walks away. The place went nuts, the people just started cheering, the screen went up, Charlie was there, everybody stood up, and the place went berserk. It was the longest standing ovation I've ever seen."

When Chaplin stepped out on to the stage after a wonderful introduction, Chaplin kept it short and sweet. "Words seem so futile, so feeble," concluding with, "You are wonderful, sweet people. Thank you." Chaplin was handed a bowler hat and cane, and attempted to mimic his old Tramp character, but the

years were clearly getting the better of him and he dropped the hat. Still, the moment was captured on film and remains one of the most touching in award ceremony history.

The Los Angeles Times published a nice article on the event: "After a 20-year exile in Europe, Charlie Chaplin returned to Hollywood to receive an honorary Oscar on April 10, 1972, for such comedies as The Kid, The Gold Rush, City Lights, Modern Times and The Great Dictator. Chaplin, then 82, received probably the longest standing ovation in the history of the Oscar telecast as he walked slowly to the podium to pick up his Academy Award for his "incalculable effect in making motion pictures the art form of the century." Chaplin was quite literally speechless as he looked at the throng of stars whose cheers kept getting louder. He finally uttered "thank you so much," referring to the audience as "sweet people." And there wasn't a dry eye in the house when Jack Lemmon gave him his famous Little Tramp hat and cane."

Chaplin met the new stars of the day and even ran into Jackie Coogan. After his moving but short speech, Bogdanovich approached Chaplin at the Governer's Ball. Introducing himself as the man he had been in touch with for the past few weeks who had put together the montage, Chaplin's only comment was "Jackie Coogan. He was a little boy and now he's a fat old man." Embarrassed, Peter did not know what else to say. Finally Oona broke the silence and said how good the tribute was. "Yes," Charlie mumbled, "yes, very good, very good."

Chaplin later wrote in his book, My Life in Pictures, that it was a touching event, "but there was an irony about it somehow..."

The same year he was receiving other honours, like the Golden Lion at the Venice Film Festival. During the event St Mark's Square was turned into a Chaplin party and they screened City Lights in the open air. Chaplin was all set up to stand on the balcony and wave to the crowd just before the film started. He was slightly delayed in doing so, having watched a bit of his film, and clearly enjoyed it, before greeting the gathered masses.

When he returned to Switzerland he started work on the book My Life in Pictures to be released in 1974. Compiling his favourite pictures, both

from his life and his movies, he wrote new captions to go under each. The book is wonderful and a perfect companion to the autobiography. The images are fabulous of course but Chaplin's memories are like little nuggets of gold. Later in the year he visited London for the launch of the book and happily gave interviews. He insisted to reporters that he would never be able to properly retire because ideas refused to stop entering his head. He was 85 at the time and sadly no more films were to come to fruition.

Then Chaplin received the news that he would be granted a knighthood. The poor little boy from London had finally made it. Reaching London with his family, Chaplin waited in Buckingham Palace as the orchestra played the theme from A Countess from Hong Kong, before going into a rendition of Chaplin's classic song Smile as he went for his knighthood from the Queen. Unable to walk all the way to Her Majesty, he was wheeled towards the Queen herself who apparently told Chaplin that his films meant a great deal to her and had helped her through the years.

When Charlie received his knighthood, film critic David Robinson was surprised to get a call from Chaplin's secretary Miss Ford: "This dragon lady who was their secretary and sort of bodyguard. They were scared of her too, she was such a dragon lady! She was wonderful. So she called me and said 'We are having a little party at the Savoy to celebrate and we wondered if you'd like to come. It's only a little get together, nothing special and mostly family, but we wondered if you'd like to come.' So I said I would very much like to come, of course, and I was there. It was a family affair, very much so. And... there he was! But by this time he was certainly declining in health and one could see the mind was going OK, even if he found it hard to communicate. He was just sitting there quietly. If you spoke to him he would not respond or even seem to hear what you said. The family knew this, so they didn't bother him and left him alone. He was sat on a sofa and I sat beside him. For most of the party we were sat together. It was very interesting because the mind was working, but when one asked him something the answer then came none. But his eyes never left this small boy, and I never

discovered whose child he was. I suppose he must have been one of the grandchildren. He was a little boy with very bright red, very curly hair. And Charlie was fascinated by him. The little boy came over and stood in front of him, and Charlie reached out with his fingers and fingered the hair. Then the little boy ran away again and Charlie's eyes followed him. And then, having been so uncommunicative, he took my arm and said 'You see, they always gravitate towards the mother.' And this was a rather startling sentence, having finding him so uncommunicative. Then there was a call from 10 Downing Street, and the prime minister asked if he might be able to come down and offer his congratulations. It was Harold Wilson, he'd actually organised the whole thing. He admired Chaplin very much. And Harold Wilson came into the room and suddenly the old Charlie was renewed. He stood up, went forward and shook the hand with a bright smile. It was an amazing transformation. And then Wilson turned to someone else and Charlie was left there and absolutely subsided again and had to be taken back to his chair. It was very sad to see his decline, but Oona was defying it and would not let anyone acknowledge that he was not what he once was. But it was very strange because that person that he had been was somewhere inside there."

Charlie then went to Anvil Studios in London to supervise the recording of the new music he had written and composed for A Woman of Paris. Given that the film had received such a muted response upon release in 1923, and that he had barely spoken of it in the following decades, it was quite remarkable that Chaplin was revisiting what many saw as a failed project. Once again, David Robinson was invited to come along, having received a phone call from Miss Ford.

"He needed a lot of help from the arranger," Robinson told me, "and they used a lot of his old music. I mean, it is certainly not one of his best scores and is not as successful, however it is his! And we went there and sat in a little observational room outside from where the orchestra was playing. Obviously he was not contributing much but he was watching with some interest. Oona and Miss Ford were there, then they went off and left us alone, just the two of us. Again he was not communicative, but again could just spark up. I tried to talk

to little response, and then I said did it take long to write the music for this? And suddenly the old Chaplin was back. He said, not long, inspiration mostly! A nice phrase. Then a daughter came in, one of the younger ones. I'm not sure which one now, but he suddenly said May I present to you, my daughter? Very sprightly. And then we sat some more and the orchestra broke and we were looking through the window at them. Then two of the musicians pretended to fight. This he found very disturbing and very frightening. He said I want to go home! I want to go home! So I went and got Oona and Miss Ford and they took him home. He was frightened."

I asked David if, even though Chaplin was but a shell at this point, he was still aware of being sat next to Charlie Chaplin, the legend himself, and whether he had an aura. "Of course he had an aura," laughed David. "Even if I invented it he had an aura. It was one of the greatest moments of my life."

In 1975 the documentary The Gentleman Tramp saw release. Featuring up to date footage of the elderly Chaplin at home in Vevey, holding hands and walking the grounds with Oona, it's a tremendously moving and heartfelt piece, essential viewing for anyone looking for a glimpse into Chaplin's later home life. The very same year Peter Bogdanovich had visited Vevey to interview Chaplin in his home about his life. Footage of this is rather upsetting to watch. When Peter brings up Mack Sennett (the man who signed him to Keystone Pictures) and Fred Karno (the man who gave him his stage break), Chaplin appeared to have no memory of them at all. He did, however, recall minute details of his tragic childhood. Even senility had not blown away the dust of those memories.

Chaplin's final months were spent relaxing with family at home in Vevey. Eugene says they often put on his old films, and whenever the children laughed at particularly funny moments, Charlie would sit upright in his chair and smile too. Eugene also said that though he had not permitted them to watch TV when they were very small, he now had a more relaxed attitude towards it. Gout limited his physical life, so he happily sat with the family watching the French news and mimicking the actors

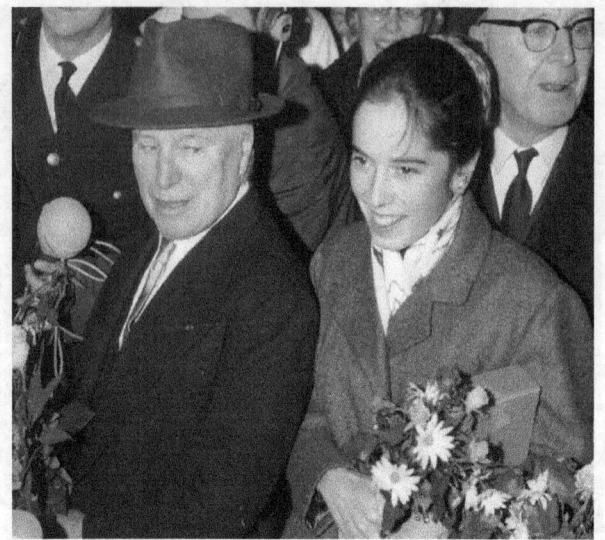

In the middle of October 1977 he made his last trip out of the house when he, his family and some local friends went to see the Circus Knie. After this he went speedily down hill, needing constant care and attention. Still, he seemed happy, most of all because Oona and the children were always close by.

On Christmas Eve 1977, Oona invited all the children that had moved away for a festive celebration at the Manoir de Ban. Michael recalls coming through the door to a mountain of gifts and a joyous atmosphere. Charlie, though not well, was sat in the corner enjoying himself. By evening however he felt unwell and asked to be taken upstairs. He also requested the door be left open so he could hear the joy of the children as they opened their gifts. The next morning, in what Michael called perfect timing, Charlie Chaplin passed away peacefully. The Little Tramp had waddled off for the final time, but he would never, ever be forgotten.

in films. Geraldine recalled he would sit before the fire, in both summer and winter, for hours. When Oona tried to get him outdoors he would often refuse and say "it's my only luxury." His last appearance on film was at the Harvest Wine Festival, where a frail Charlie in large black rimmed spectacles smiles as the children frolic. Other times he sat for hours with Oona, often not saying a word but always holding hands. The driver would take them to the river, where the happy couple would relax until sundown, when they would be taken back to the Manoir de Ban. It seems to have been a peaceful, even idyllic final chapter in the great man's wonderful life.

CHARLIE CHAPLIN

AT MUTUAL FILMS

After enjoying two years as the world's most popular cinematic comic, Charlie Chaplin, already with a vast number of films under his blest, went over to Mutual Films. In 1914 he had signed to Mack Sennett's Keystone Film Company, making roughly a film a week before heading over to Essanay Films where his work began to take on more sophistication. It was in 1916, when aware that he was outgrowing the confines of Essanay that he looked ahead and agreed to make a series of pictures for Mutual. Chaplin's work then took on true brilliance, a run of 12 films which, for my money, are among his finest. After fulfilling his contract with Mutual he went on to make A Dog's Life and other shorts under First National before embarking on his feature length classics, starting with The Kid and The Gold Rush. But the Mutual Films deserve a place of their own in the Chaplin canon as pure gold...

MUTUAL CHAPLIN SPECIALS

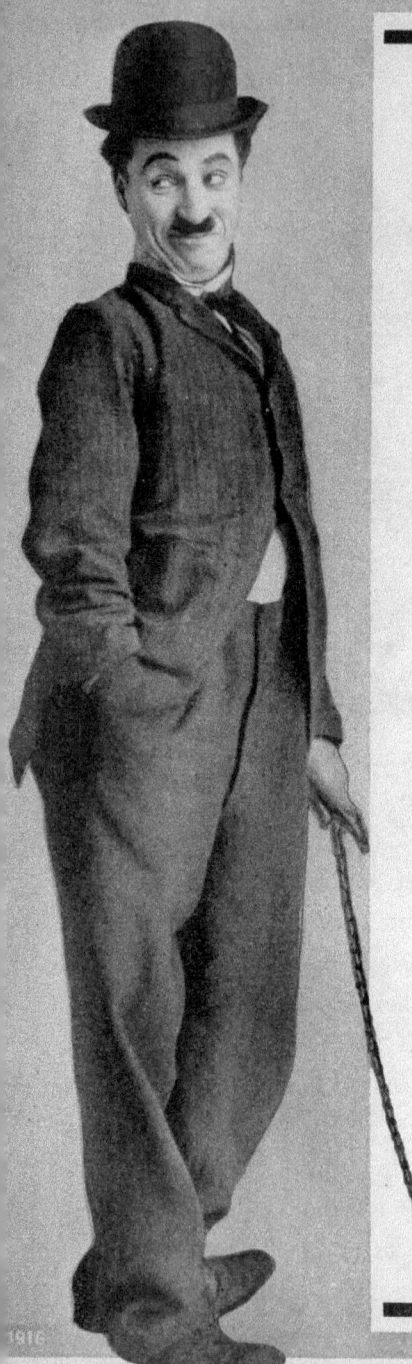

The Greatest Attraction

At this particular season of the year, during the torrid days of summer, the strongest possible attractions are needed to hold up patronage.

CHARLIE CHAPLIN

in the series of Mutual Chaplin Specials is the surest and greatest attraction you can book. **Remember, a Chaplin Mutual has never failed to fill any house!**

His latest subjects, "The Floorwalker," "The Fireman," and "The Vagabond" are drawing record breaking business everywhere and leave such a delightful impression that everyone is eagerly following his Mutual Chaplin releases.

Book the entire series of Mutual Chaplin Specials at any one of the 68 Mutual exchanges.

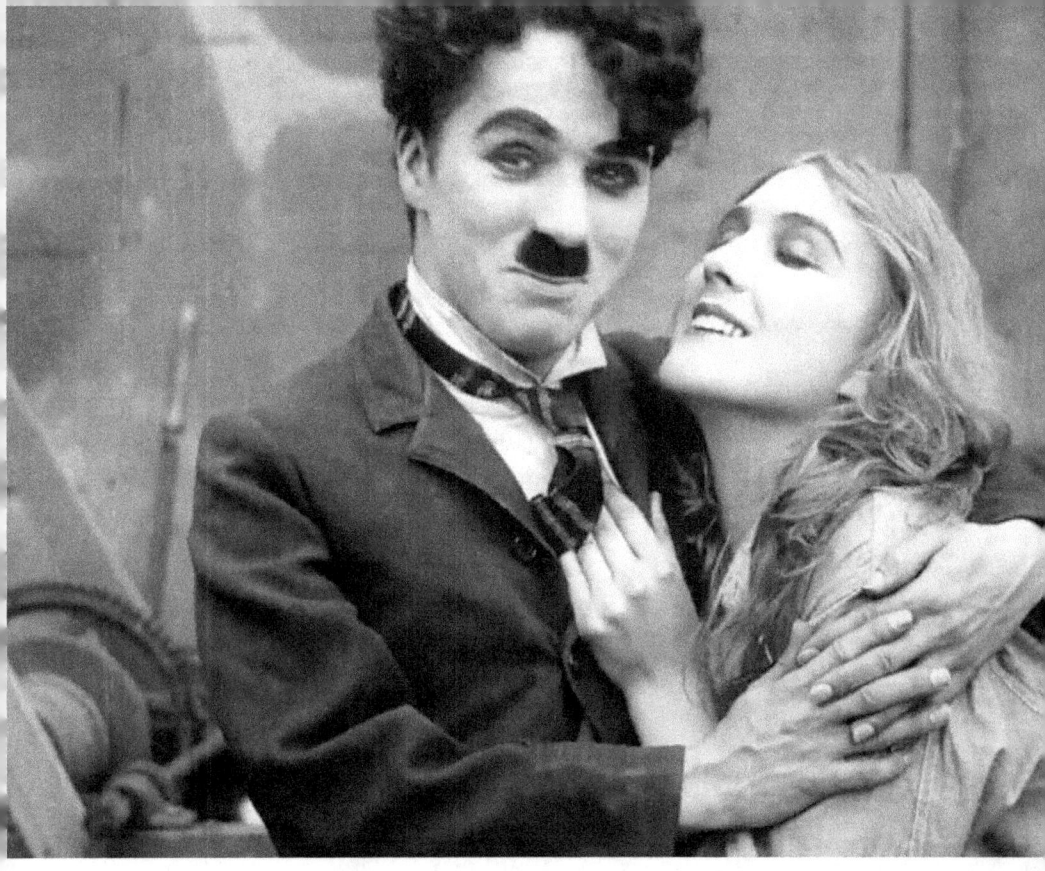

THE FLOORWALKER (1916)

And once again, Chaplin moved on. For a man becoming increasingly famous and adored, the world itself seemed too small for him. Signing over to Mutual Films in 1916, Chaplin was at his early height, though he would only go up in the world as the year went on. Not only was he the world's biggest film star, he was also one of its leading filmmakers, a man taking cinema into new territories. At only 27, he was now being paid $670,000 a year (a deal worth 10 million today), keeping full creative control over his work and having a full studio to himself, the famous Lone Star, made by Mutual especially for Chaplin. The pressure was off in some ways, especially considering that it took Chaplin nearly two years to finish his 12 Mutual films and the studio had no choice but to be patient. But Charlie was under great pressure in other areas, especially when one considers the enormous weight of having to provide the goods, to come up with new ideas all

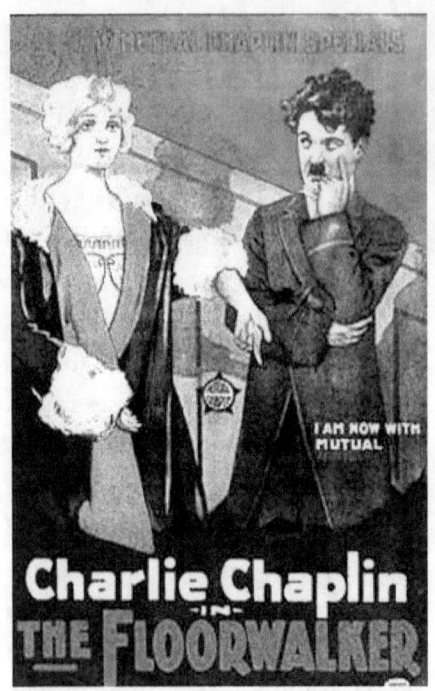

Charlie Chaplin
-IN-
THE FLOORWALKER

I AM NOW WITH MUTUAL

the moustache, but won't stick so closely to the other clothes. It'll depend on what the circumstances [of the story] demand. It isn't how one is dressed, but what one does and how. Slapstick comedy has as much artistic possibility as the best efforts from the stage."

Chaplin was keen to change the scenery and if not all the costumes, then at least a bit of them. He now wished to push his Tramp persona into new areas, a variety of plots which offered endless opportunities. He had his then girlfriend leading lady, the ever reliable Edna Purviance, as well as his trusty cameraman Roland Totheroh. Feeling confident, Chaplin went to work.

Chaplin's first film for Mutual was The Floorwalker, another huge leap for Chaplin as a filmmaker and comedian, and pretty innovative for its time, especially in the comedic genre. The movie itself follows Chaplin, once again shining as the Tramp, making his way through a department store, and generally causing as much trouble as one little fellow possibly can. Eric Campbell plays the store manager who, with the help of a co-worker who resembles the Tramp, plans to rob the store. Of course, Chaplin ends up getting

the time. Working days often had Chaplin sat in a corner, thinking up new gags and plot devices, while everyone just sat around waiting for the gold. Genius, then, had to be worked at. He also had the Chaplin fame to deal with, the constant adoration and pestering by the public.

Ever the professional, Chaplin ensured his public, and himself of course, that work was his primary focus, not fame. "I'm going to make better pictures than I did last year. I am doing my own scenarios and my own directing. I'll keep

wrapped up in the chaos, firstly as an accused accomplice then as the film's unlikely hero.

At 24 minutes, Chaplin excels at ensuring the viewer never gets bored, even when very little seems to be happening. For fans of Charlie's general clowning, this film is a real treat. It moves fairly slowly, and lingers long on Chaplin as he acts the fool around the store. The camera work is simple enough, staying flat at all times, as in Chaplin's early films, but it works tremendously well, ensuring that every moment and gesture is clear as day. The film is one of those Chaplin classics famous for its various set ups rather than the whole of itself. The presence of the escalator for instance was comic genius at the time, and the various shenanigans involving it in The Floorwalker still raise laughs today. Perhaps even more well known, and much copied, is the so called "mirror" scene, which features Charlie and his lookalike, both dressed in near identical garb, mirroring one another's movements. It became one of those classic scenes often paid homage to, firstly in Max Linder's Seven Years Bad Luck, then by the Marx Brothers in their seminal comedy Duck Soup, and thereafter in countless cartoons and comedies. Again, as with many cinematic devices which became very familiar to the public at large, the foundations of the gag itself were all Chaplin.

And The Floorwalker, pretty much, is all gags. There is a thin plot, but it's mainly an excuse for Charlie to hang a series of physical showstoppers on. There is no pathos, and the Tramp of the Floorwalker is not someone to be pitied or loved as he would be in later, and indeed some earlier, films. What comes out from this film though, and its rich and packed 24 minutes, is that Chaplin is entertaining to watch no matter where he is or what he is doing. As in other Mutual films to follow, Chaplin is the centre piece. He could put the character and himself in all kinds of settings, but the effect would always be the same; the little fellow remains the focal point.

That said, the supporting players are also extremely good. The bright and always watchable Purviance is as wonderful as ever, and Eric Campbell, Chaplin's favourite bad guy in the Mutual years, is almost as effective as Chaplin. Contrasting his brutish

temperament and imposing size with Chaplin's meeker manner and lighter build, they make a brilliant on screen duo, whether fighting or merely arguing amidst the twirling chaos.

Though it stands still emotionally, and the viewer does not feel a lot of warmth for the Tramp (even though we admittedly enjoy his escapades), The Floorwalker illustrates how in control and on top of his game Chaplin really was when he signed up with Mutual. As his time there went on, he would expand in other areas, perfecting the art of filmmaking, tightening his control over the public, and seeing his Tramp persona become cinema's greatest character.

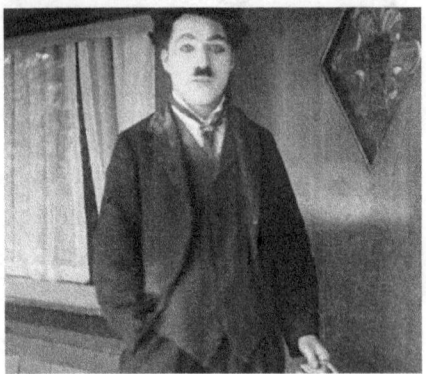

POLICE (1916)

Even though Chaplin was already enjoying his new found freedom at Mutual, Essanay still had one more movie of his to release. That movie was Police, which surfaced in May of 1916, and concerns the Tramp being released from prison and falling straight into a scam involving an imposturous parson who takes all of Charlie's money. Chaplin then gets convinced into doing some burglary, which obviously goes wrong when Charlie misses the finer points of breaking and entering and simply opens the front door. His ineptness however charms the house owner, Edna Purviance, who ends up covering for Charlie when the cops arrive, though the Tramp is not out of trouble just yet.

Police is another modern satire from Chaplin, albeit a subtle one, and stylistically it pre-dates Modern Times and the likes in its dealings with class and social hierarchy. With subtext aside, Police is simply an enjoyable comedy, crammed full of laughs and expertly played out routines. For me, once again, the most charming aspect is the relationship between Charlie and Edna, which blossoms in the film's second half, only to be interrupted by the pesky law. Chaplin's direction is efficient too, bringing the viewer within the

unfolding action, with a generous helping of close ups and changes in perspective which ensure the tale remains engaging from first frame to last. There are some great sequences too, such as the fruit stall fiasco, complete with ass kicking, and the breaking-in scene, with Charlie and his criminal chum Wesley Ruggles making a great bumbling double act. Again, Chaplin gets a great feel for this "alternative" way of life, conjuring up the sheer desperation so evident in society's outsiders and the rustic, run down locations in contrast to Edna's more refined living standards. As expected from Chaplin, there is much more than comedy here.

Reviews were good at the time, which must have irritated Chaplin given that the film took some attention away from his current Mutual work. Motion Picture News wrote, "Those who believe that Chaplin's abilities are limited to the mallet, the kick and the spinal curvature walk, should see this picture. They will be disillusioned. They will see a touch of heart interest just at the end of the subject, and they will see that Charlie's stock pantomime includes pathos as well as fooling. But of course, the picture is mainly clever horseplay, beginning with Charlie's exit from prison, and ending with his flight from a policeman."

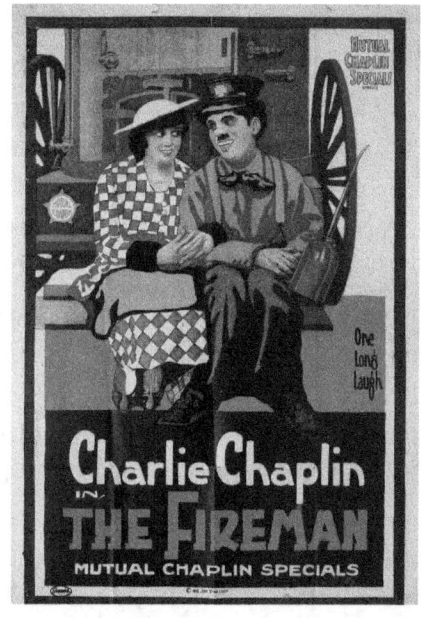

THE FIREMAN (1916)

Chaplin's second film for Mutual was The Fireman, released in June of 1916, in which Chaplin displayed his ineptitude while working with the fire fighters at Station 23 and getting entangled in a risky con. Eric Campbell is the chief who has an arrangement with Lloyd Bacon, who intends to burn his house down in order to collect the

insurance money and hand over his

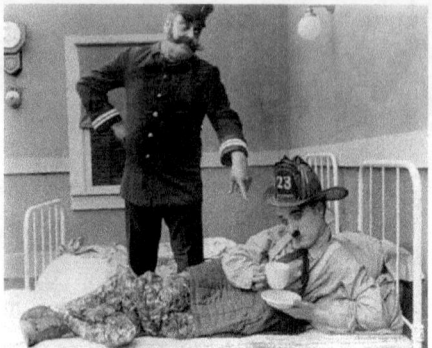

daughter, Edna Purviance, to marry him as a thank you. Their scheme could have come to fruition had they not come across Charlie, who also has eyes for Edna and is intent on being her hero, this time not in his day dreams, but in the real world.

The Fireman was shot at a real fire station at South Western in LA, which was good news for Chaplin and Mutual's budget, seeing as the props were all ready to use at no extra cost - even though the fires started at derelict buildings added extra expense. The film certainly looks good, but personally I feel The Fireman is one of the least accomplished of the Mutual movies. With its primitive gags and broad delivery (Eric Campbell is especially cartoonish in this one), it would have felt too old fashioned even during his Essanay phase and fit more snugly in to the Keystone era. The film is nicely done, with direction kept simple, performances suitably wacky and gags coming thick and fast, but save for a few technical advancements (the reversed film etc.) The Fireman has nothing beneath its surface to warrant analysis. If Chaplin were going for a straight comedy for once, sidelining pathos and depth, he had succeeded. As it is today though, a newcomer to Chaplin might be led down the wrong path by the shallower humour on offer here, and be put off exploring Chaplin's more complex, emotional work.

One wonders if reviews like the one written in The Chicago Tribune influenced Chaplin's decision to move from broad slapstick, albeit slowly, towards something more substantial. "There is more of soup-spilling and Keystone kicking than is necessary for successful slapsticking," the Tribune complained, before adding, "but there is also a certain novelty of situation and a jolly humour in its expression that moves to much mirth. Charles Chaplin is a true comedian who doesn't need to resort to the conflict of the physical to make fun. He has a sufficiently mobile expression to do that."

If Chaplin didn't take reviews seriously, then he certainly took notice when it came to fan letters. After The Fireman came out he was sent a letter by a long term but concerned admirer, a note which has gone down in Chaplin legend and which Charlie himself famously kept. It read: "I have noticed in your last picture a lack of spontaneity. Although the picture was unfailing as a laugh-getter, the laughter was not so round as in some of your earlier work. I am afraid that you are becoming a slave to your public, whereas in most of your pictures the audience were a slave to you..."

Though Chaplin was admittedly ego-centric, and obviously had a lot of self belief, especially when it came to his work, he was not closed minded or too sure of himself to ignore feedback from a paying punter. It's hard to imagine a popular star/director today taking a single fan's view seriously (or even reading the letter in the first place), but Chaplin was much more than a mere celebrity - he was an artist. And though one can't say he strived for perfection, due to that strange enigma's elusiveness, he was very concerned with delivering the best work he could, if not only to justify the huge sums of money Mutual were giving him, then for himself and his audience.

THE VAGABOND (1916)

It was clear when he emerged with his next film, July 1916's The Vagabond, that Charlie Chaplin took on board the feedback of that one fan who thought he was repeating himself and relying too much on his past work. Though its location and setting was inspired on a comedic level, The Fireman had been something of a tired retread back into old ground, while The Vagabond was completely fresh, beautifully poetic and among the best films Charlie had made up to that point - which is quite a lot when you line up that filmography.

In many ways, The Vagabond is almost like a follow up to The Tramp, and not only because Chaplin's lovable little fellow was back at centre stage. Stylistically, in its presentation and tone, it shared the pathos and sad humour of the earlier film, but The Vagabond is also its own film completely. This time, the Tramp is a musician, a violinist in fact, who early on in the film has an unfortunate encounter in a bar with

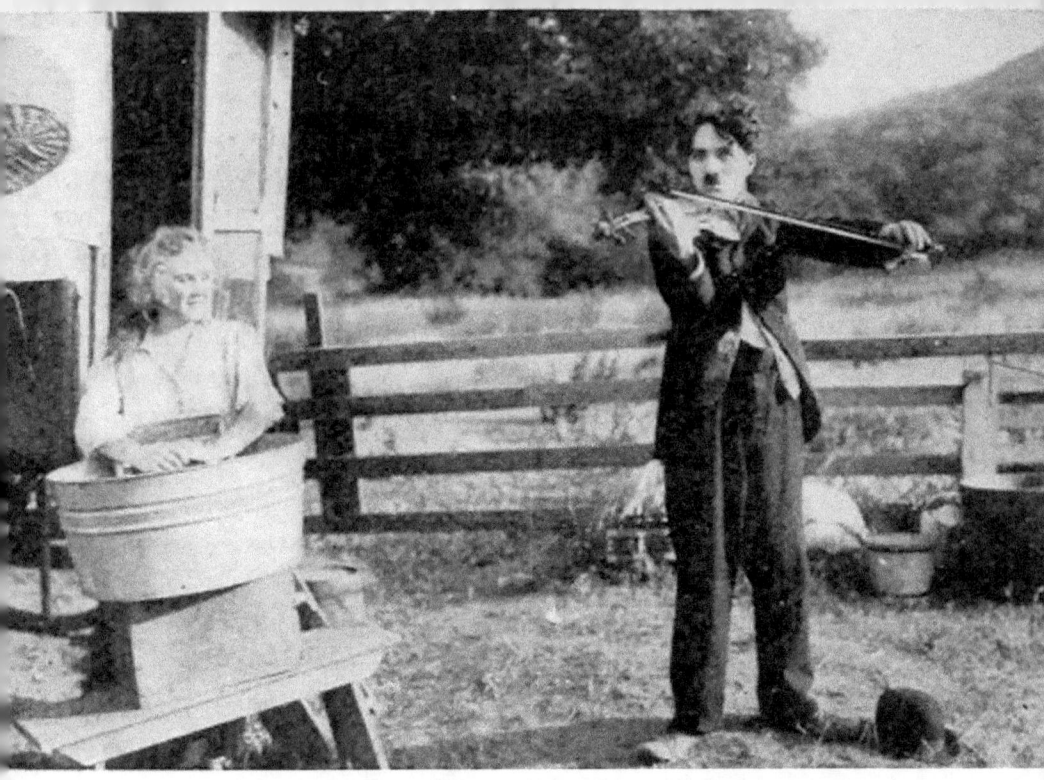

some competitive musicians. The film really gets interesting when Charlie leaves the dingy bar and heads outside, where he comes across a gypsy caravan. Here he meets the beautiful Edna Purviance, a downtrodden gypsy who enjoys Chaplin's violin playing but is dragged away by her cruel captor, Eric Campbell, who having kidnapped her, has her living a slave like existence. Thankfully, Chaplin is feeling brave and decides to step forward and rescue this fair maiden. After beating up her vicious keeper, Charlie and Edna ride away in the caravan and wake up the next day in a new life together. While Charlie makes some morning breakfast, Edna goes out to collect water. There she meets an artist and, quite quickly, ends up as his muse. A jealous Charlie finds himself sidelined in this new romance, and feels bitter given the circumstances of her escape from the gypsies. In the end however, despite leaving for the artist via limousine and being reunited with her mother for a "better" life, she realises Charlie is her true love and rushes back to the battered old caravan to embrace him. It's a rare happy ending for the Tramp, this time with no underlying sadness.

The Vagabond is, in short, a mini masterpiece. Chaplin's Tramp was so fixed in the world's collective mind by now that any scenario featuring him was bound to grip them from the start. When he enters the film, feet first I might add, as seen below the saloon doors, one can imagine the collected applause of many millions of moviegoers, content that their unlikely hero, the little fellow, had arrived on screen for his latest adventure. Chaplin is always brilliant of course, but here, as the Tramp yet again, desperate for any money he can raise with his sad violin, our hearts are his from the word go. We are on his side, plain and simple.

In the old Keystone days, The Vagabond would have surely stayed there in the bar. At this stage however, countless films into his career, mere bar room antics would have quickly become tiresome, and Charlie just may have received another letter from that most critical of fans. Wisely he decided to shift things away from the familiar. The Vagabond swiftly, four minutes into the film in fact, moves towards Edna. After his pub trouble, we see Edna's mother (in a nice, smooth side tracking shot) holding a picture of her lost beloved daughter, then cut to Purviance herself being manhandled by the vicious brute who has abducted her. Charlie mounts a fence and comes across this pretty woman, run down by her treatment, and opens his heart to her. The attraction and chemistry between the two comes exploding off the screen. Indeed, Edna says more with a glance and a slight smile than most modern actresses can do with a full scene of dialogue.

When Charlie puts it on himself to be her hero, the film takes a sharp turn. The contrast between Campbell's huge bulk and Chaplin's diminutive scrawniness raises a laugh, and naturally ensures we goad on his inevitable victory all the more. When they ride away triumphantly, one cannot help but be overcome with emotion that Charlie and sweet Edna are on the road to freedom. Chaplin, clever as always, then takes us on yet another twisted turn when we might least have excepted it, slipping away the joy we felt for Edna's escape from underneath us and making the Tramp a figure to pity when she meets another man and seemingly forgets about Charlie's brave kindness. Again though, ever the sensationalist to have us laughing one minute and

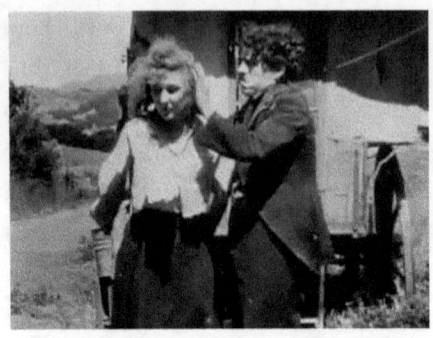

weeping the next, Chaplin ensures the little fellow gets the girl. It's one of the most enthralling of Chaplin's early films (all this in 25 minutes or so!), with one of the most gratifying of finales.

All the elements in The Vagabond had been present before in Chaplin's best work before this, but The Vagabond feels like a step up. There is some fine slapstick early on, the obligatory daftness of that era of silent comedy, but the film then ensures we invest our hearts in the fate of the Tramp and Edna. She plays it wonderfully too, which helps a great deal, and there are genuinely touching moments between the pair; when he washes her face for instance, it's very moving.

Chaplin doesn't so much as manipulate our emotions, but leads them with developments so complete it's hard to resist, heading straight to the places he would like them to go, though he does so with such delicacy that we far from object. Indeed, the Tramp is sympathetic, so much so that it's impossible to dislike him. The way Charlie plays the jealous guy when she clicks with the artist is tastefully done too; so subtle in fact is his acting that we never feel like we *have* to be on his side, but rather choose to be. There is a great sequence when the artist and Edna are really connecting over the dinner table and a rather foolish Chaplin uses the tablecloth as a bib, acting more like the infant child with the two adults. Chaplin times it perfectly, as he does with all the film's vital moments. The careful acting ensures that, while the film is undoubtedly old fashioned, it is never corny, and we buy every second of Charlie and Edna's winding love story. It's played straight faced, without unnecessary dramatics and flamboyancy in the gestures and movements. Charlie was becoming a master of understanding his craft, and the audience who had paid to come and see it.

As actor and director, Chaplin arguably had done nothing better than The Vagabond up to that point. Though there were inspired moments in many

works before it, there is a flow and togetherness about the film that ensures, for me at least, it established itself as a new high for the rapidly improving artist. The direction is similar to previous films, but it seems somehow sharper and straighter to the point, never indulging in fanciness for the sake of it and being very much *for* the film in keeping with its brisk pace. Chaplin once described a film as a tree, one which you must shake to remove all the dead weight. This theory is proven correct with The Vagabond.

In 2015 the BFI, who have released sublime editions of the Mutual movies, claimed The Vagabond to be Chaplin's first masterpiece. On their website, Graham Fuller writes, "Easy Street and The Immigrant are generally regarded as the best of the Mutuals. Almost as famous are The Pawnshop, for its plethora of visual gags, and The Rink, for the Tramp's trouncing of the black-socketed heavy Eric Campbell on roller skates. Yet there's a case to be made that The Vagabond, Chaplin's third Mutual film and a reworking of his Essanay release The Tramp, was his pivotal work of the period – and his most touching."

Even fans of the film however have criticised aspects of The Vagabond; the happy ending for one is seen as a cop out (though it wins me over every time) and the idea of the Tramp settling down with Edna's upper class family, and them accepting him, is hard to swallow. Chaplin did apparently write an alternative ending where he tries to kill himself after being rejected by Edna by jumping into a river, but as no footage exists of this sequence David Robinson, the finest writer on Chaplin there is, says it's another Chaplin myth and should not be taken so seriously. It's plain to see that for once, for whatever reason he had, Chaplin wanted an upbeat ending, a traditional finale we might have seen in more straight forward dramatic films of the time. But for me it works, though I do love a downbeat Chaplin ending, pathos and all, as much as the next fan.

ONE A.M. (191

The difficulties in writing about a popular figure, especially when one is a big admirer of the subject, is trying to keep ones opinions as unbiased as possible. When assessing the work of Charlie Chaplin, someone whose work I

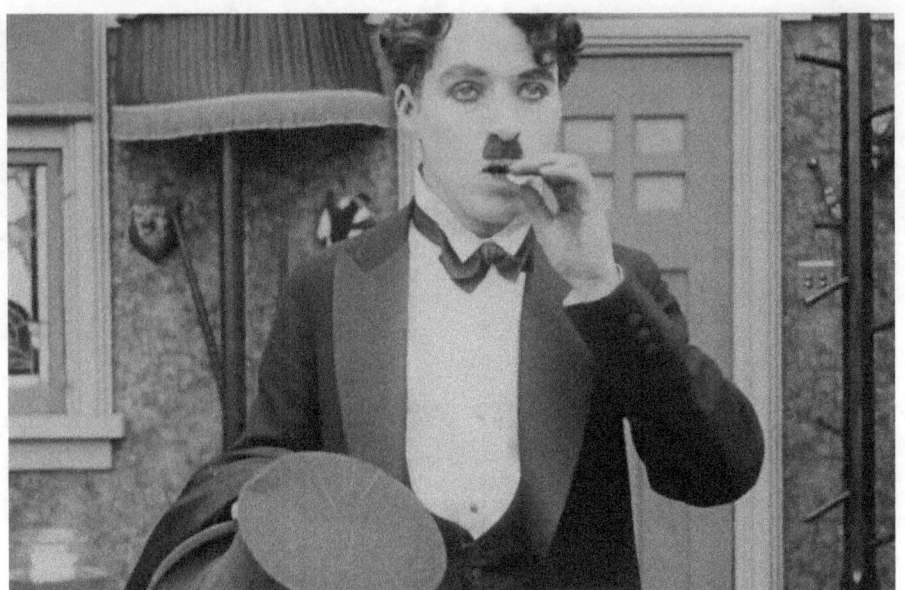

adore, it is equally challenging not to over enforce my own opinions of each film on the reader. Given that I have my favourites and am not an academic writer, the book, against my efforts, will naturally become clouded by preferences. That said, I need to come out and declare unashamedly that One A.M. is one of my very favourite Chaplin films, either full length or short.

This 27 minute gem has no plot at all, and features, apart from a driver in the first minute or so, only Charlie Chaplin himself for the whole film. The basic premise, as plain and uninteresting as it seems on paper, features Chaplin as a wealthy drunk, arriving home and being unable to get to bed. He firstly struggles to get through his front door, eventually climbing in the window when the door knob becomes too much of a challenge for him. Once inside, there's the tricky matter of the dual staircases to deal with. Chaplin attempts to scale the steps on numerous occasions but repeatedly fails, and even ends up with the carpet wrapped around him. (This minor set back, however, does not prevent him from pouring himself another drink.) There are multiple, seemingly endless set ups for Chaplin here, each one as hilarious as the last. When he gets his

cloak caught on the circular table, it becomes a rat race to reach the decanter. When he comes up with the genius idea of getting on the table to ascend the stairwell, he is trapped in a scurry resembling a hamster in its wheel, running wildly on the revolving surface like a drunken clown.

Other stand outs involve Chaplin wrestling with stuffed animals, climbing up the hat stand and falling about the place in increasingly adventurous ways. When Charlie finally makes it upstairs, he has the erratic Murphy bed to deal with, which springs independently up and down, back and forth, making it impossible for the inebriated Chaplin to get down for a proper night's sleep. Eventually, he settles for the bath, using the matt as a cover.

First and foremost, this film is a showcase for Chaplin the physical comedian and is a perfect chance for him to illustrate his genius not only with the props around him, but with his own body. Though heavily padded, it's a miracle he didn't hurt himself repeatedly plummeting down the stairs, but it's a credit to his nimble, balletic movements that he keeps getting back up unscathed for the next pratfall.

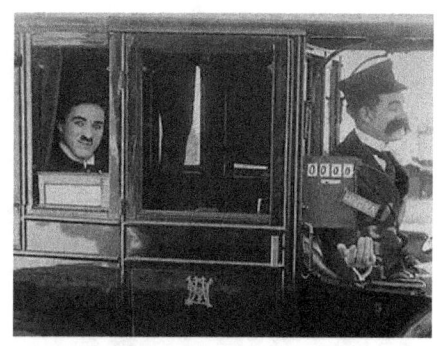

We all know how Chaplin suffered in his childhood, but we are also aware that he absorbed a lot of the behaviour of the London characters he saw every day in the streets, particularly the drunkards. Here, clear from the first frame, Chaplin has not only soaked up all those inebriates, but also every drunk scene he had played on stage and screen himself up to that point, first with the Karno act, then with Keystone and Essanay, before joining Mutual, the studio where he would hone his craft. It's an amalgamation of all his finest drunken work, every fall and stumble a mini work of art in itself. Only Chaplin could make being drunk a thing of genius.

As director, with the help of Roland Totheroh, Chaplin was one of the few filmmakers redefining the rules of cinema, thinking up and executing new ways to make the best of a scene. Whether it was a long shot or a half

close up, Chaplin seemed to know the right place for each. Though the British technical innovators of late 19th century and early 20th century cinema had toyed with close ups and perspectives, these men were all but forgotten in a matter of years. Chaplin then, along with the likes of D.W. Griffith, was one of the rare breed who was attempting something outside the box. Granted, One A.M. stays near enough at a straight-on perspective, as if we the viewer are seated in a theatre watching a stage performer do his thing; but there are close ups too, such as when Charlie is wrapped in a carpet, and the camera does move and follow him about the stage. We, naturally, are drawn to him, watching his every move in the strange, almost surreal surroundings he is struggling with.

What makes it even funnier is that Chaplin the drunk never gives up. He could, and perhaps should, just flake out and go to sleep there on the ground floor. But he is stubborn, denying there is a problem and seems intent on getting to bed. It's almost out of spite, refusing to lie down and give in. Chaplin himself said as much in a 1918 article for American Magazine: "Even funnier than the man who has been made ridiculous... is the man who, having had something funny happen to him, refuses to admit that anything out of the way has happened, and attempts to maintain his dignity. Perhaps the best example is the intoxicated man who, though his tongue and his walk give him away, attempts in a dignified manner to convince you that he is quite sober... this attempt at dignity is funny."

Chaplin is right, and anyone who has ever been drunk knows all too well the feeling of attempting to keep one's dignity when so inebriated it's a challenge to merely stand straight. That Charlie's "drunk" (as he is credited) still manages to retain his dignity and air of self respect, even when being sprung about on a malfunctioning bed, or wrestling with a stuffed cat, is a credit to his performance, not merely the hilarity of being a drunk in denial.

Funnily enough, for such a well received short, Chaplin thought it was a misfire. In David Robinson's book on Chaplin, Robinson himself comments that the film was a daring display of virtuosity, but also added that Chaplin himself commented, "One more like that and it's goodbye Charlie." What he

meant by this is unclear, but it's notable that Chaplin stayed away from sole comedies again, re-employing his supporting players from the next film onwards.

David Thomson wrote an interesting observation on Chaplin, singling out One A.M. for his insistence that Chaplin's wildly out of control ego could have led him to self destruction and isolation. "The worldwide appeal of Chaplin, and his persistent handicap, have lain in the extent to which he always lived in a realm of his own: that of delirious egotism. Is there a more typical or revealing piece of classic Chaplin than One A.M., in which he exists in virtuoso isolation, executing every variation on the drunk-coming-home theme? It is like a dancer at the bar, confronting himself in a mirror."

I wonder if Chaplin knew that a one man show brought too much attention to his self absorption; or maybe secretly he hated bearing the sole responsibility and being the focal point to the millions of viewers all over the world. Reviewers did applaud his efforts, but Photoplay were quick to say, "Come on back Edna", a demand which perhaps caught Charlie's attention. Ego stroking or not,

filmed theatre or no-frills cinema, it's early Chaplin at his most inspired, entertaining, and perhaps most importantly of all, funny.

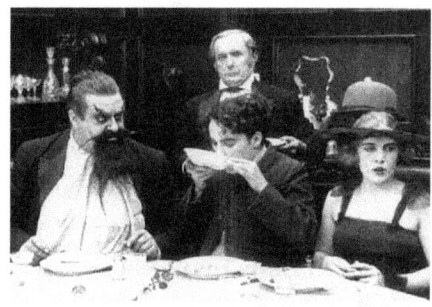

THE COUNT (1916)

Chaplin's fifth film for Mutual was The Count, in which Charlie hung up the Tramp persona for a moment and played the assistant to a tailor, played by Eric Campbell. The plot concerns Charlie accidentally burning the trousers belonging to a well known Count, and getting fired. Campbell finds a note inside the trousers, an invitation to a party, and decides to go along. Charlie attends it too, fighting with his former employer for the hand of Miss Moneybags, played by Edna Purviance. One farce after another occurs, resulting in the real Count turning up and the speedy exits of Campbell and Chaplin.

For Chaplin, coming off the sole success of One A.M., The Count was very much a return to familiar territory. Once again he was with trusty cast members like Purviance and Campbell, and given plenty of opportunities to draw parallels between certain levels of wealth and class, while providing the obligatory laughs in between. My favourite scene is when they are all sitting down to dine, and Chaplin eats the watermelon, so big it covers his whole face and he has to clean his ears out with a napkin after devouring it. To isolate other moments seems futile, for The Count works as one long, neatly unfolding story; yet the dance hall sequence, with Charlie showing his physical versatility, balletic in its awe inspiring beauty, is undoubtedly one of the most memorable from the early days, sticking out as something quite special. (One must also note that lovely zoom as Charlie and Edna leave the ball room, and the camera follows them outside.)

Eric Campbell is here perfect as the burly counterpart to Chaplin's weasel-like rascal. Though Chaplin worked opposite many authority figures in his career, few could provide the menace and overpowering power like Campbell. Again though, I must confess it's the warmer, cosier moments with Edna that work the best, though here she is not the earthy victim ready for Chaplin to rescue her, but the well-to-do rich girl, way out of Charlie's social league.

At the time people saw it as a return to the fully casted slapstick farces the world had come to love him through. Chicago Daily News wrote of the film, "Charlie Chaplin, millionaire movie man who cavorts for your pleasure if you have a dime, ambled into view as a bogus count today and raised peels of laughter from the loop to the limits. All of which is sufficient to indicate that Charles is back with some of his old time slapstick work that will chase the blues and make you forget to speculate on the probable length of the war."

THE PAWNSHOP (1916)

The Pawnshop is vintage Chaplin, one of his most popular early films and surely a trademark movie that, if you were a newcomer to Chaplin, would be a good place to start. As one should expect, it is full of laughs, and has a seemingly endless amount of superbly timed and

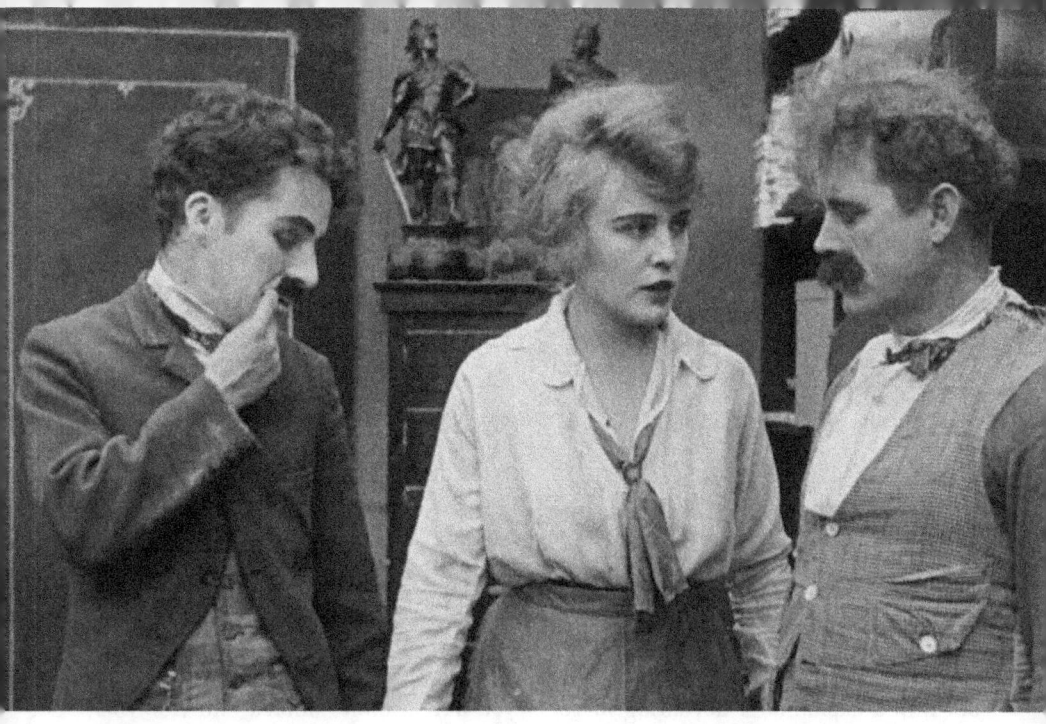

figured out comic set ups. Though it may be stating the obvious, Chaplin is simply wonderful in it, coming up with one great gesture and gag after another. In the light of such films as The Vagabond it is low on pathos, which is, though a loveable trait in Chaplin's movies, potentially off putting to someone not attuned to Charlie's methods. Indeed, The Pawnshop is classic slapstick, lacking the often irritating predictabilities of Keystone, but bearing all the stronger points of his Mutual and even his Essanay works.

The Pawnshop was made during a rough patch in Charlie and Edna's off screen romance, and though they made up and retained their intimate relationship for the time being, it was clear that they would not last forever, even if their working relationship remained as solid. The Pawnshop is gag packed, a straight forward affair with Chaplin playing a bumbling shop assistant who has his eyes set on Edna, the boss's beautiful daughter, and ends up stopping a robbery of the store. Like The Count, it lacks the emotional punch and sentimentality of The Vagabond, but remains a reliable stand out from his shorts.

Apparently the shoot was a loose and fun affair, with the cast and crew waiting for Chaplin, who finally arrived with a

pile of notes and announced, "Ladies and gentlemen, we are about to open the pawnshop!" The Pawnshop is clearly one of those films born out of Chaplin's long strolls, his intense sit downs in the studio, wracking his brains for new scenarios and gags. That he was still able to come up with the goods after making some 56 films already in a mere two year span is quite extraordinary. Not a moment in this fine two reeler feels forced or clichéd; in fact it's funny, energetic and hugely entertaining all the way through.

The setting of the pawnshop, like the fire station before it, was an inspired choice, and there are plenty of tools and props at Chaplin's disposal to wreak havoc with. He does so imaginatively, creating some of the most memorable moments from his early years. Who knew one could get so many laughs out of a ladder? The excellent alarm clock scene still gets a lot of credit from critics, but my personal favourite moment is when Edna, looking striking, interrupts the fight between Chaplin and his co-worker, calling the man a brute and Chaplin "a mere child". Chaplin hilariously plays the upset innocent, but subtly checks out Edna's rear every time she looks away. This is subtle humour ahead of its time in my view and still hilarious today.

In simplistic terms, Chaplin's early work can perhaps be divided into two categories, the pathos heavy Tramp tragi-comedies and the light and playful workplace farces, with Chaplin taking on every possible job role with equal ineptness. Here he is at his most ludicrous and useless, and the speedy, unstoppable pace makes for fun viewing. It's classic slapstick, no more, no less; so sit back and enjoy it.

BEHIND THE SCREEN (1916)

Chaplin had given us a glimpse into the making of a movie before, namely in His New Job for Essanay, and in A Film Johnnie, which presented movies from the view of the audience, but in Behind the Screen, his seventh Mutual film, he showed us what it was like to be an underling behind the scenes on a film set. Chaplin plays a prop man called David, an assistant lugging gear around in preparation for filming. As this is Charlie we're talking about, he's pretty useless at his job. Eric Campbell plays Goliath, his superior, constantly out to

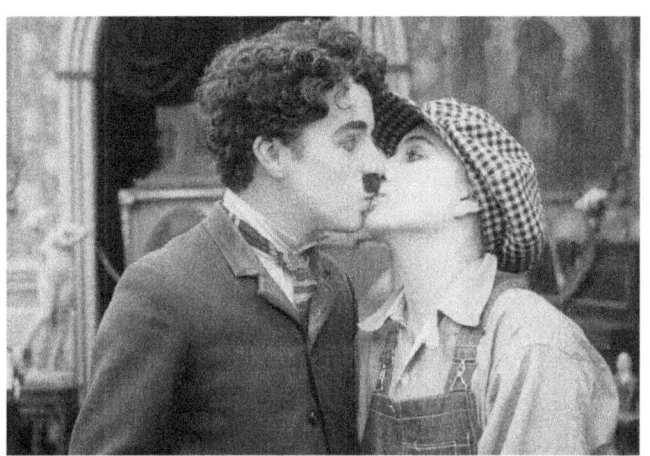

People have spoken of Chaplin's knack at transforming objects into others, as the Surrealists were to do a few years later in their art (indeed, Chaplin was thought of rather highly by Andre Breton and many Surrealists, including Salvador Dali, as was Buster Keaton), and Chaplin is highly inventive here in that field. There are some lovely scenes in the film elsewhere, including the one where a disguised Edna in flat cap shares a kiss with Charlie (presumed by Campbell to be a homosexual kiss, judging by his subsequent mock-prancing, which irritates Chaplin no end), and the whole custard pie fight remains a stand out, clearly a nod to the primitive gags of his days at Keystone.

make Charlie's life as difficult as possible, while Edna Purviance plays a naive young woman hoping to start a career as an actress.

The film opens with some wonderful slapstick scenes before going off into a plot involving a strike, where the workers plan to blow up the studio with dynamite. That said, the plot is rather inconsequential in this one, for the most enjoyment is had in sitting back and enjoying Chaplin's intricate routines and farcical mix ups. For my money there are some of the funniest and most surreally inventive Charlie gags in this 24 minute short, including the scene when the boulder keeps falling down and when Charlie gathers all the chairs on his back and begins to resemble some kind of demented hedgehog.

Chaplin did a lot of work on Behind the Screen (he was taking a lot of time over films by this stage, much longer than he had at Essanay) and Kevin Brownlow was the man to unearth the various outtakes from the film, which were used in his Chaplin documentary Unknown Chaplin. One of the cut scenes

involved an axe narrowly missing Chaplin's toes, which Charlie filmed backwards for safety reasons. Quite why he cut it from the film is anyone's guess, but Charlie, never one to waste a good gag, must have had his reasons.

As the First World War raged on, Chaplin kept working and knocking out top notch comedies, which were much needed in such dark times. The self referencing, in-joke laden Behind the Screen is by no means among his finest work, but it's breezy, light and very enjoyable indeed.

THE RINK (1916)

It's fair to say that once Charlie came up with a good scenario and setting for a film that the ideas, with careful thinking of course, began to flow quite naturally, and that he usually filmed them in the order the concepts and gags came into his head. The Rink is one of those films which must have clicked quickly for Charlie, given that the skating rink had such potential for great slapstick comedy. This unfussy two reeler is in many ways a stop gap for Chaplin, creative in its own way but mainly relying on his physical skills, though

remaining totally pure for that reason alone. He did not need to turn to pathos or sentimentality here; Chaplin merely let the rink inspire him in his outrageous clowning.

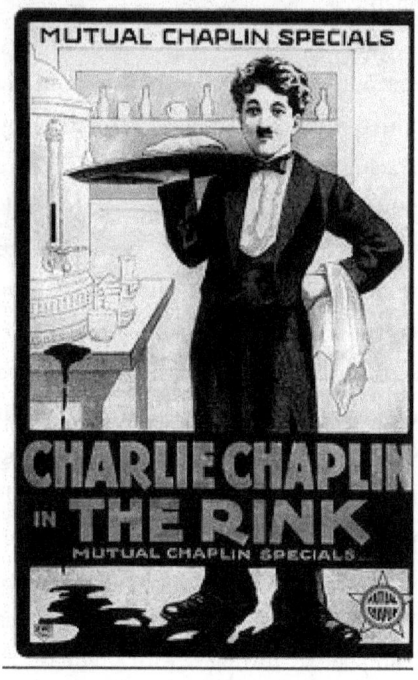

Chaplin plays a typically inept waiter who unexpectedly transforms into a highly talented skater at the rink. He has his eyes set on a local girl, played by Edna Purviance of course, and gets a bit of trouble from Eric Campbell's Mr Stout, but putting these minor aspects aside the film is mainly enjoyable for observing Charlie's balletic skill. Indeed,

though he garners many laughs with his clumsiness, he is magnetic viewing when skating. It's no surprise to learn that Chaplin apparently put the professional skaters hired for the film to shame.

Edna herself has a nice role in this, and is blessed with the first scene in the film, where she awakes her father by placing a kitten on his face before telling him she is going to the rink. Charlie's scenes at the restaurant are wonderfully done, and one could have certainly enjoyed a full film in this setting. By now though, Chaplin had developed many of his films to be split into two sections, the first building towards the second, and in The Rink this practice is at its best, the film taking on a new life once he dons the skates. Whether bumping into the mountainous Campbell, flirting with Edna or gracefully gliding across the screen, Chaplin is hypnotically brilliant throughout. But Charlie saves the best till last; the final chase scene, which unexpectedly leaves the rink and goes into the street, is the highlight of the film, an example of Chaplin surprising us once again and pulling out all the stops.

The Rink, Chaplin's last film of 1916, was hugely popular in its day. Reviews were mixed, though Variety loved it, writing: "All in all The Rink averages up well with the best work he has done for the Mutual". Moving Picture World were more critical: "Chaplin at the rink is amusing enough, but such a vast amount of material is needed to keep a swift farce constantly on the move. While Chaplin works hard and seems to stand the strain of being funny, an awful strain in its way, he is not given much new opportunity."

EASY STREET (1917)

The New Year got off to a great start for Chaplin when Mutual released his latest film, Easy Street, an excellent two reeler which has proven to be one of the most enduring comedies he made for the studio. It begins with a down on his luck, extremely glum Tramp lying in a heap next to a Hope Mission, which he then enters. Inside he sees Edna Purviance, who urges him to join her in her work. Instead, Charlie heads to the police station where he's seen an advert looking for new recruits. They hire him immediately and send him on his way to

140

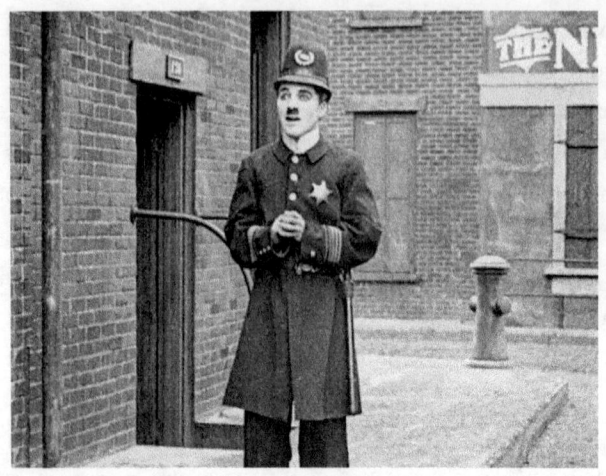

up Easy Street by thrashing all the lowly down and outs into submission.

Easy Street ends on a high after spending most of its time under a dark cloud of violence and depravity, when a New Mission opens up in the street and we see former reprobates heading down

his beat, the lawless and terrifying slum that is Easy Street. The first moment illustrating his new authority comes when Chaplin heads outside and a man on the street mocks his ill fitting attire - so Charlie knocks him out with his truncheon.

His first job at Easy Street is to break up a fight, and he finds himself faced with the hugely intimidating Eric Campbell, who Charlie ends up defeating, after quite a struggle it must be said, by smashing a street lamp and knocking him out with its lethal gas. They meet again later in the film, while the Tramp also rescues Edna from a fiend, but ends up sitting on the drug addict's needles which gives him super strength, as well as the ability to clean

to better themselves. For the most part however, Easy Street is extremely raw and near the knuckle, especially for a comedy. Once again this was new ground for Chaplin, and Easy Street, with its drug references and brutality, could not have been more different to his last picture, the breezy The Rink. Clearly, Chaplin was not content with resting on past laurels and providing mere slapstick to his hungry audience.

For Chaplin, this was a backward look towards his troublesome, tough childhood in London, while he also drew inspiration from old acts he performed while still under Fred Karno. The film is full of inspired moments, especially the gaslight incident, which manages to be both slightly shocking and extremely

funny. When I met with David Robinson, he said the set Chaplin built for Easy Street was a carbon copy of the kind of streets Chaplin would have roamed as a boy in South London. A walk round the east end proves this.

While Chaplin recreated the location of his poor childhood, he also managed to conjure the desperation so prevalent in late 1900s London. Though he does turn his life around in Easy Street, at the start of the film the Tramp is at his most lowly; he's practically lying in the mud and even steals money from a collection box. Yet we understand and grasp his neediness, his hunger, his total and utter helplessness. Carefully, Chaplin had built the Tramp up in previous movies so that by now we can accept anything he does. Even the violence he inflicts on the creeps at Easy Street is perfectly acceptable in our eyes. He has transformed himself into a kind of demented, violence loving mutation of a Keystone cop, but he is acting for the greater good. Though Chaplin had explored this area in his earlier film Police, which he shot for Essanay, Easy Street is a much more accomplished work. It has a moral centre which validates the lunacy on display, and actually heads to a positive conclusion.

While he was making Easy Street, Chaplin had also been working on his abandoned feature Life, which seems to have been aiming at the heart wrenching tragicomedy of The Kid. The poverty and ugliness he wanted to depict in Life ended up, for the time being at least, in the authentic grittiness of Easy Street. Though his work had often been raw before this, Easy Street seemed to get it all right, and while still comic, seemed to be more of a serious statement on poverty and injustice, hidden beneath the Tramp/Chaplin formula the world was so used to. This time, the Tramp does not toddle off on his merry way despite the shortcomings his life continues to present him with; here he not only restores himself, transformed as he is into a man of the law, he also restores justice, dragging Easy Street and its occupants up from the mud and into a more pure, holy and decent way of life. Perhaps Chaplin was dreaming, hoping, that he could have done such a thing during his desperate London childhood.

Easy Street is among the very finest of all Chaplin's early short films, and leads

the viewer into the more complex, emotional and thought provoking works of the 1920s and beyond. It is a pre-echo of what is to come.

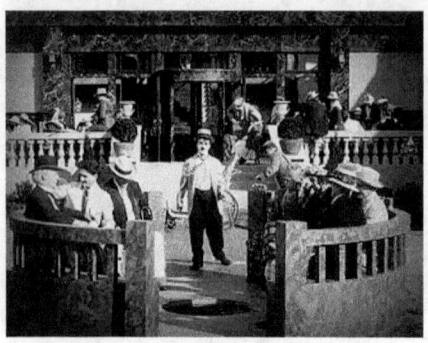

THE CURE (1917)

The Cure is another reliable and unsurprisingly funny Chaplin two reeler, with him playing on his old drunkard routine to great comic effect once again. This time he's an inebriate who books himself into a health spa to clean up, though one could say he wasn't exactly committed to the idea seeing as he smuggles in a suitcase of alcoholic beverages. Once inside he runs across Eric Campbell, suffering from gout, and is charmed by Edna Purviance, who urges him to give up the demon booze.

The Cure was a film Chaplin apparently thought highly of. It was made at his Lone Star Studio at the peak of his powers while Mutual were still being patient with him and the time he was taking over new product. It's light, crammed full of superb gags and though offers no social satire and lacks pathos, so strongly defined in Chaplin's finest work, it's a film which moves swiftly and effortlessly, due to the constant firing of jokes. It's genuinely funny, and Charlie is hilarious throughout, something which Chaplin's doubters deny he was capable of being. His harshest critics may accuse him of relying too much on schmaltz and sentimentality, but they may be surprised at viewing a film like The Cure and witnessing how straight forward funny he was.

The Cure was released three months after Easy Street in 1917, and it was another film born out of endless re-shoots and re-thinks, with Chaplin trying and trying again until he found the right gags and executed them to his satisfaction. In Kevin Brownlow's documentary Unknown Chaplin, we see The Cure being assembled bit by bit, while the clapperboard indicates takes in the high seventies, with elements still, even at that stage, being shifted, fiddled

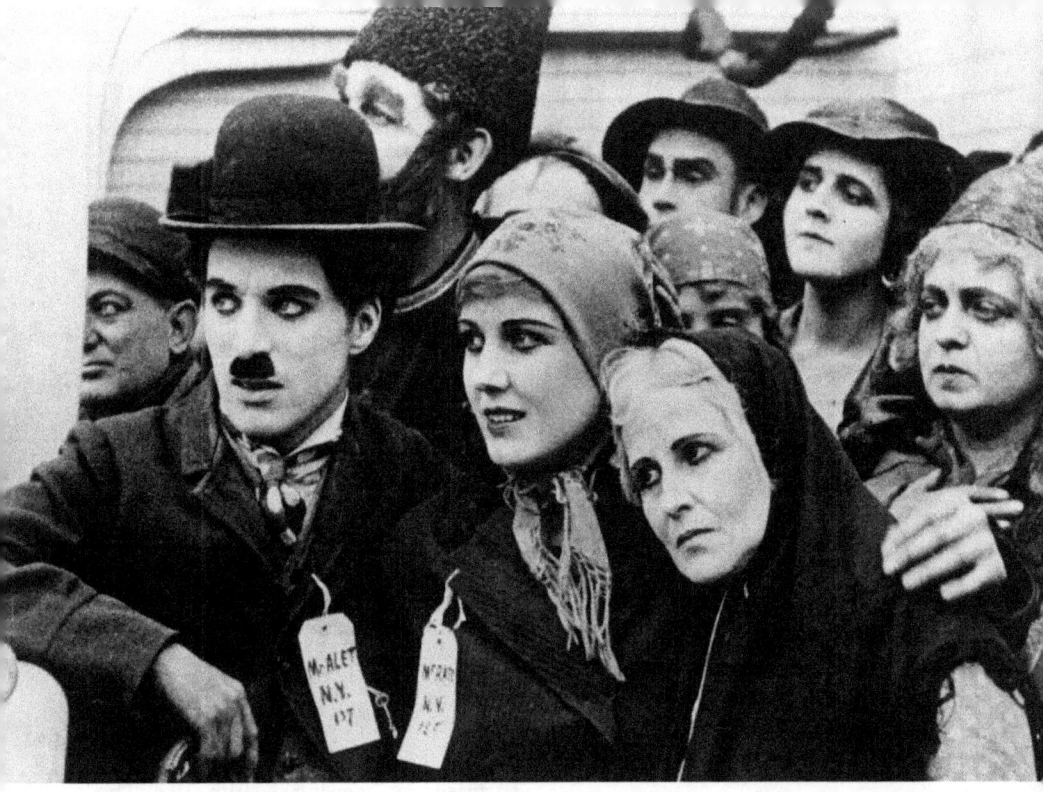

with and removed by an experimental Chaplin in search of the perfect gag.

It took four months to make The Cure, which when compared to Chaplin's days at Keystone and Mutual was a shooting schedule to rival Stanley Kubrick at his most meticulous. Judging by reports of this period, Chaplin was becoming more moody and unpredictable on set, but one must consider how stressful his working life must have been. Chaplin films may look simple to modern viewers used to CGI overload, but as Geraldine Chaplin once noted, the work that went into these movies was almost superhuman. Though he had a hard working crew and

talented cast at his disposal, Chaplin had most of the pressure sitting on *his* shoulders. Adding together the unprecedented fame he was experiencing, life could not have been so easy for Charlie Chaplin in 1917. That said, these constraints are not evident when viewing the care free, laugh-a-second delights of The Cure, one of Chaplin's most enjoyable comedies.

THE IMMIGRANT (1917)

Like many of Chaplin's strongest shorts in the Mutual years, The Immigrant can be divided into two segments; the first

involves Charlie on board a ship heading for America, while the second sees him poor and run down upon his arrival. The heart of the picture, with gags aside, is his interaction with Edna Purviance, who plays a fellow immigrant in search of the American dream and sadly loses her mother along the way. There are many laughs to be had, especially on the boat with its constant rocking motion, and then in the city, when Charlie struggles to pay for his and Edna's meal at the restaurant, but it's the chemistry between Chaplin and Purviance that ensures this works so well. It's considered to be one of Charlie's best from the Mutual period, and I have to say I can see why. For me, it's one of the most effective films of his whole canon.

The Immigrant began as an idea Chaplin had about Parisian bohemians. He was quoted at the time as saying, "This theme offers scope for the sentimental touch which somehow always creeps into my stories. The trouble is to prevent that touch from smothering the comedy. There is so much pathos in the lives of all true bohemians that it is hard to lose sight of it even for a moment and the real spirit of that community is far too human and deeply respected by the world at large for me even to think of burlesquing it."

Chaplin developed the cafe scene first, which was shot and re-shot numerous times with different actors and gags. Eventually, after many takes, it wound up close to what ended up in the film. He then worked on the first segment of the film, inspired by his own feelings of being an immigrant and first setting foot on US soil. The boat sequences are hilarious; the constant rocking motion of the vessel has the expected effect on the stomachs of its passengers, Charlie included, but Chaplin does get lucky and catch himself a fish. He goes inside and dines with his fellow immigrants, first laying his eyes on Edna's character. Credit must go to Purviance for being believably loveable as the object of his desires, with her appealing smile and knack of downplaying scenes to avoid melodrama. The card game, in which Chaplin wins the money he will place in the pocket of Purviance, also provides some daft humour to balance out the pathos.

As appealing as the boat segment is, for me it's the second half, with the chaotic, farcical dining scene, which

culminates in a hurried, impassioned marriage between the pair, which really lifts this into the highest section of Chaplin's filmography. All the elements are here, as they would be in other films, but somehow in The Immigrant they are all aligned perfectly, and the film works especially well. The fact that Chaplin worked and worked at a scene until it fulfilled its potential and achieved the desired effect does explain why his best work gets to you like an arrow through the heart, in that the master knows all too well how the film will affect the viewer. We may have been manipulated, but the movie is so enjoyable and moving that Chaplin is absolved. While it does have its humour, this is more a heartfelt tale of love than a slapstick gag fest, and it's all the more rewarding for that. In the three years he had been making films, not only was Chaplin continually coming up with fresh ideas, he was advancing as a filmmaker and artist, reaching the kind of heights no one had before, emotionally at least, and perhaps are never likely to ever again. Everything Chaplin fits into The Immigrant, despite it only being 22 minutes long, is stunning, while it never feels remotely over-stuffed.

And Charlie himself was rather fond of the film too, writing in his splendid autobiography: "The Immigrant touched me more than any other film I made. I thought the end had quite a poetic feeling. Even in those early comedies I strove for a mood; usually music created it. An old song called Mrs. Grundy created the mood for The Immigrant. The tune had a wistful tenderness that suggested two lonely derelicts getting married on a doleful, rainy day."

Chaplin had reached what many would call perfection, and he would do it again, the ever expanding genius defining what film's potential really was, in the truest and purest of forms.

THE ADVENTURER (1917)

Charlie Chaplin's final film for Mutual was The Adventurer, a film that was as sharply funny as The Immigrant was moving. Gag filled from the word go, The Adventurer showed that Chaplin was still very capable of making an all out comedy. There was a minimum of pathos this time, with Chaplin cast as an escaped convict on the run from the

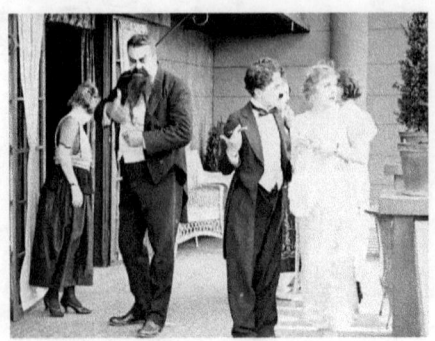

prison guards, clad in that very familiar striped jail uniform. The chase sequence takes place on a beach, with Chaplin scurrying around to flee the guards, up mountains, down cliffs and along the dusty sand. After rescuing a woman (Edna Purviance) and her mother, but irritating the girl's companion (played by the mountainous Eric Campbell in his last film before his untimely death in a car crash later that year), Charlie finds himself in their lavish home, dressed in striped pyjamas which he at first mistakes for prisoner's garb. He gets dressed up for the family's party, and realises Edna's father is the judge who sentenced him to his prison term. He vaguely recognises Charlie, but fails to identify him right away. In a farcical frenzy, Chaplin is finally recognised and then attempts to flee the party. Nippy and wily as ever, Charlie the convict gets the better of them.

Charlie was keen to move on from Mutual, and was heading to First National, perhaps using the prison as a metaphor for his feelings at the time, and the partygoers as the film business suits who saw Charlie as a commodity. But Chaplin worked hard on the shoot and it shows. The chase sequence alone took 200 takes, while it's been noted that he struggled through a lot of the film to come up with inspiring gags - though it's fair to say he got there in the end. Though he had his off set pressures, and was receiving a lot of criticism for not enlisting in the war effort (Chaplin's defence, as he wrote to a fan, was that the world needed him more for his films than they did for his fighting ability), Chaplin pulled things together and crafted a sharp, neat, straight to the point comedy, a film that does not challenge or emotionally affect the viewer, but has them laughing along with the convict's shenanigans. The Tramp may have crossed over into being an all out lawbreaking villain here, but he was still loveable, which of course is the key to Chaplin's mysterious appeal.